The Girls' Guide to Tarot

Kathleen Olmstead

ILLUSTRATED BY
SANDIE TURCHYN

Sterling Publishing Co., Inc.
New York

Library of Congress Cataloging-in-Publication Data available

Illustrations from the Rider-Waite Tarot Deck®, known also as the Rider Tarot and the Waite Tarot, reproduced by permission of U.S. Games Systems, Inc., Stamford, CT 06902 USA. Copyright © 1971 by U.S. Games Systems, Inc. Further reproduction prohibited. The Rider-Waite Tarot Deck® is a registered trademark of U.S. Games Systems, Inc.

1 3 5 7 9 10 8 6 4 2

Published by Sterling Publishing Company, Inc.
387 Park Avenue South, New York, N.Y. 10016
© 2002 by Kathleen Olmstead
Distributed in Canada by Sterling Publishing
c/o Canadian Manda Group, One Atlantic Avenue, Suite 105
Toronto, Ontario, Canada M6K 3E7
Distributed in Great Britain and Europe by Chris Lloyd at Orca
Book Services, Stanley House, Fleets Lane, Poole BH15 3AJ,
England
Distributed in Australia by Capricorn Link (Australia) Pty. Ltd.
P.O. Box 704, Windsor, NSW 2756 Australia

Manufactured in China

Sterling ISBN 0-8069-8072-9

CONTENTS

INTRODUCTION

What does the word Tarot mean to you? Are you picturing an old gypsy woman — scarf on her head, large gold hoops hanging from her ears — sitting with a crystal ball and a deck of cards? This is how most of us first hear about this ancient art. And as is often the case with stereotypes and information handed down through television and comic strips, it is misguided. It makes for a great story, but that doesn't mean it's the whole truth. Most of us have not encountered the Tarot firsthand. It's something in books or movies or that other people do. The assumption is that you have to go to an expert — someone at a psychic fair or a woman named "Mrs. Hope" who reads palms, tea leaves, and Tarot in her front room. Nothing could be further from the truth. You can consult the Tarot yourself — with nothing in hand except a deck of Tarot cards and this book. Of course, having another perspective is important and sometimes the advice of others is just what we need, but it's a mistake to think that someone else has all the answers. The ability to use your intuition and to effect change is within you. The Tarot will help light your path.

Despite what you might have heard, the Tarot will not reveal your future. There isn't one thing that you should become, one path that is available, or only one choice that is right for you. The difficulty is in seeing all the options. The Tarot helps you cut through the excess to find what is important. Ask a question, focus on the cards, and the answer will arrive in the spread. This isn't magic, though. It requires work and dedication to understand the cards. The Tarot is a guide to finding the answers that are already inside you. It provides insight into the world around you so things will seem more clear.

Hopefully, you will look at this book as a beginning — a journey that doesn't end when you turn the last page. You will never reach a point where you know everything that there is to know about Tarot and the 78 cards that make up the deck. Eventually you will know your favorite spreads by heart and won't have to look up card meanings every time, but the Tarot will never stop showing you something new — often a new way of looking at things. How could there be an end point? Insight and focus will lead to discovery.

You need to make the Tarot your own. If it makes you feel better dressing in long flowing scarves while reading, then by all means do it. The important thing is that you involve yourself with the Tarot and learn from the experience.

HISTORY

The origin of the Tarot is uncertain. We know that the first mention of it occurred in 1392. The court records of King Charles IV of France say Jacquemin Gringoneur was paid money to produce three decks. No one suspects that Gringoneur was the sole creator of Tarot cards, though. They were probably well known by the time the court requested their own copies.

How do we know that? First, it seems unlikely that one person could have created such an elaborate card system on a King's whim. It is so involved that there must have been a predecessor. Second, the Marseilles deck, another famous set of Tarot cards that didn't appear until the 17th century, is generally believed — by examining colors, design and costumes — to depict characters from the early 14th century. These images predate Gringoneur's cards. So historians theorize that the Marseilles deck was copied from a much earlier one that has since disappeared. So, the question remains — where did these cards, and their design, originate?

One of the most popular theories is that the Gypsies brought them to Western Europe. This nomadic group is thought to have journeyed from ancient Egypt (thus the name "Gypsies") carrying the cards containing the wisdom of Egyptian mystics. The trouble with this idea is that the Gypsies actually came from India and didn't arrive in Western Europe until the 15th century. In other words, the cards got there first.

Some historians believe that Tarot was a way for a persecuted people to record their beliefs without fear of discovery. It would have been much easier to transport a deck of cards than a book. It contained no words, only pictures, and was, therefore, able to pass on information in a society where few people could read. "Ars memorativa" (the *art of memory)* is a philosophy stating that pictures arranged in a specific order can be used as memory devices (known as the study of mnemonics). Break a story into sections — stanzas, verses, beads, or cards — with every fifth or tenth one containing a special image or marking, and it opens up entire avenues of hidden thought and memory. The images would speak for themselves, so members of the persecuted group could maintain their cover. The threat of punishment, imprisonment, or death was very real, and in the years before the cards first appeared, several groups — the Gnostics, Cathars and others — were considered heretics and executed for their beliefs, which ran contrary to the church's doctrines.

Other students of the Tarot claim that a strong connection exists between the Tarot deck and the mystical Jewish book, the Kabbalah. There are 22 letters in the Hebrew alphabet (like the 22 cards of the Major Arcana in the Tarot) — and each letter has its own special significance and position on the Tree of Life. This Tree does not contain words but graphics — ten points that lead from new beginnings to the final Kingdom (much like the ten cards in each suit in the Minor Arcana). The Kabbalah is undoubtedly an attempt to preserve knowledge, so many believe that the Tarot might have originated in the same way.

Could any of these groups have been responsible for creating the Tarot cards? Whoever was, they did a fine job of hiding their tracks and throwing pursuers off their trail.

The three decks that Gringoneur painted for the King of France, as well as the Visconti deck created thirty years later by Bonifacio Bembo for the Duke of Milan, were used for entertainment purposes. It is said that they were called the Tarot because there was a card game popular in Italy in the early 15th century (the time of Bembo's design) called the Tarocchi.

Take a look at the playing cards of today. Do you see any similarities to the Tarot deck? The 22 cards of the Major Arcana have disappeared, but the four suits of the Minor Arcana are still in use — Wands became clubs, Pentacles became diamonds, Swords became spades, and Cups became hearts. The Fool has been transformed into the Joker and the Page and Knight have combined to form the Jack. If you've ever seen Italian playing cards you will have noticed an even stronger resemblance. The deck is much smaller, but the original suits of Wands, Cups, Swords and Disks (Pentacles) remain.

The mystical qualities of the cards seem far removed from today's decks, though.

As early as 1420, card games, gambling, and fortune-telling started to be denounced as "tools of Satan." People began to distance themselves from this unrespectable pastime.

It was about this time that the Tarot came to be associated with Gypsies and fortune-telling. Until the 18th century, when mystical groups such as the Masons and the Rosicrucians began to study the Tarot in earnest, there was little mention of the cards except in connection with Gypsies. But even though it was considered immoral or indecent, people still sought out fortune-tellers, sometimes calling them to their homes for readings. It was as irresistible then as it is now. (Of course, today we realize that it isn't our future that the cards reveal — but the many layers of our past and present.)

The study of the Tarot reached a new level in the 19th century when a French Rosicrucian named Eliphas Levi discovered the connection between the Tarot and the Kabbalah. Interest in the Tarot continued to grow and reached a new peak in 1888 when The Order of the Golden Dawn was founded in England. This group formed to study occult and mystical arts. Its existence was short — only fifteen years — but its impact was impressive. A.E. Waite, the author of the deck used in this book, was a member, as were many important Tarot scholars that we know today — Paul Foster Case, Aleister Crowley, MacGregor and Moina Mathers. The Order claimed to have access to secret oral traditions and the keys to understanding the Tarot. New decks using ancient symbols and designs were created and made accessible to the public. It was largely through the effort and education of these men and women that the Tarot moved into public consciousness.

As the years passed, more people picked up the Tarot and claimed its power for their own. The language has altered and numerous designs and specialized decks have appeared, but the message has remained the same. There are decisions to be made every day — some big and some small — that determine the paths we take in life. Through insight and discovery we can all achieve our goals. We simply need to be reminded that the answers are inside us always.

USING THE TAROT

A Quick Step-by-Step

The Tarot deck contains 78 cards. It is divided into two sections — the Major Arcana and Minor Arcana.

The **Major Arcana** has 22 cards — numbered 0 to 21.

The **Minor Arcana** has 56 cards — divided into 4 suits.

- ◆ The suits are Wands, Cups, Swords, and Pentacles.
- ◆ Each suit contains 14 cards — numbered Ace to 10, then 4 Court cards.
- ◆ The Court cards include Page, Knight, Queen and King.

There is a procedure to the Tarot and it needs to be followed. As you become more familiar with the cards, you will personalize the readings with your own understandings, habits, and preferences, but don't stray too far from the basics. The Tarot is fun, but it's not a game. You need to treat it with respect if you want to get good results.

All of these steps will be discussed in greater detail later on, but here's a quick outline:

1. Set the mood for your reading. Get comfortable and relax.
2. Think of a question or wish.
3. Choose a layout that works well with the question (some are more general than others).
4. Shuffle and cut the deck. Clear your mind of everything but the question.
5. Lay the cards out in the pattern of the spread.
6. Read the cards starting with Position 1.

After all of this, it's up to you. Record your thoughts in a journal, write a song about it, or stand on your head while reading the cards. It really doesn't matter, as long as you treat the process with respect and stick with its basic rules.

One of the first things you need to do is sit down and familiarize yourself with your deck of cards. You don't have to memorize the meaning of each one (that will probably happen naturally) but it will help in your readings if you recognize the pictures and symbols. This is the initial step in establishing a relationship between yourself and your cards.

Pick a card — any card — to carry with you all day

This is a simple exercise to learn about a new card each day. Carry a card with you every day. Put it in your backpack or purse or tuck it away in your journal. This is a great way to learn about the deck and each card. And the idea is also to learn a few things about yourself.

There are two ways of choosing this card:

- ◆ Lay the cards out before you face up. Spread them out and look at them closely. Take your time and choose the one that stands out — whichever one attracts you the most.
- ◆ Or you could pick one blind. Give yourself up to fate and take a chance on what you are given that day.

In either case, don't expect that this card will guide you through the day. It is

something for you to think about, to wonder how it applies to you and the world around you. Let's say that you picked the "Temperance" card, which signifies moderation and clarity. Watch for times during the day when these qualities come into play.

Say there's an argument at school between two people. How would moderation help this situation? If neither person reacted in an extreme way (getting angry and fighting rather than talking it out), chances are it would be a very different day.

Record all this in your journal. Make an entry in the morning (or whenever you pick the card) and one at the end of the day — a before-and-after shot. Ask yourself:

Did you make assumptions about what the day would bring based on the card?

Did any of them come true?

Were you surprised by anything?

Is there another way of looking at the situation now that you have the time to stop and think about it?

What are the other meanings of the card and how does that affect what you observed or experienced during the day?

Picture Perfect

The secrets and information of the Tarot are communicated through pictures. The best way to learn and understand the meaning of each card is to study the images. Before you read the interpretations in this book, look over each card —

examine it carefully — and record your reactions and thoughts. These will be the most important interpretations you'll ever find. They will help you develop a relationship with the deck of your choice. Whenever you sit down to a reading — no matter how long you have worked with the Tarot — don't immediately consider the interpretation of the cards. Take in the images and ask yourself what first comes to mind when looking at the whole. Connect with the complete picture before you start to take it apart. Each reading is a new experience. Never assume you know your response beforehand.

Destiny? Do you choose the cards or do the cards choose you?

There are two ways of looking at "the choosing of the cards."

The first is that the card you pick is the one that is meant for you. Of all the combinations possible, this is what you are supposed to see on this particular day at this very time. Yes, this is what many people would call destiny — that the cards choose you as much as you pick them. Remember though, that "destiny" doesn't tell you how to read the cards. Which interpretation should you choose? How does this card apply to your life? The ball is always in your court. Whatever part destiny and fate may play in those cards being laid before you, they still only provide clues. The rest is up to you.

The second view is that every card has potential meaning for you. It wouldn't matter which one you pulled from the deck — it would relate to your life in some way. The deck represents your life and all its possible combinations — big and small. You have to move through the deck slowly because you can't deal with them all at once. Sometimes a reading will be monumental — the shake-you-in-your-boots kind of feeling. Other times it might prove only mildly interesting — like a generic horoscope on a bad day. If we were "head over heels" every day, we would think "head over heels" was ordinary and start looking for something else. This is a good reminder that the little things in life are just as important as the big ones.

Picking a Deck

This is no easy task because there are a lot to choose from. The Rider-Waite — also known as the Waite-Smith — that illustrates this book is the most popular deck today, but is by no means the only one. Do you like cats? Well, there's the "Cat Lover's Tarot." Perhaps you would prefer a deck using characters and images from the *Lord of the Rings*. There are some that reproduce medieval or renaissance era cards or royal courts. There are Native American Tarot cards and Goddess-centered cards, even a round Mother Earth deck. You can find almost anything to suit your tastes.

Most Tarot books use the Rider-Waite deck because it is the most common and uses the most straightforward images. This doesn't mean that it is the deck for you

— but it's a good place to start. Also, in many places, the Rider-Waite deck is the only one available.

Only you can decide what is best for you. If the choice is there, take your time, go with your feelings, and pick a deck that resonates with you.

Caring for and Storing your Cards

Keep them someplace safe, dry, and secure. Tradition says that they should be wrapped in silk or cotton (both are natural fibers), but that isn't necessary. This is your deck of cards and you should decide what works best. It's a good idea to have someplace special to store them, though, such as a bag or special box (maybe something you make yourself, see page 116), or you could wrap them in a clean towel or pillowcase. Perhaps you have a favorite t-shirt that is too small — but you don't want to get rid of — that you'd like to donate to the cause.

The idea is to preserve the energy of the cards. Keep them separated from everything else.

Who Handles the Deck?

Many people believe that you and only you should handle your deck. They say this establishes a relationship between you and the cards so that the mingling of your energies will guide the reading. Therefore, no one else should lead a reading with your deck or use the cards. The only exception to this rule is when you are reading for another person (the Querent) and he or she needs to shuffle.

It's up to you. How do you feel about the energy of the cards? Will you read the cards just as well if someone else has used them? Just in case you are worried, there is a way of clearing the deck.

Clearing the Deck

Shuffle the cards after a reading, then restack them in their proper order:

1. Start with the Major Arcana — 0 Fool to 21 World (stack them face up so lowest card is on the bottom). We always start at the beginning and count up.

2. Separate the cards by suit and place in this order.
   a. Wands
   b. Cups
   c. Swords
   d. Pentacles

3. Within each suit — start at the Ace and finish with the King.

When you've finished, put the cards back in their storage place and leave them for a while. This will restore their energy so you can start fresh.

The Ins and Outs of Asking a Question

You can ask the Tarot anything you'd like (as long as you're prepared for the answer), but there are a few tricks to the way you ask them.

First of all, it's best to ask a specific and direct question. Limit your question so that the answer will be more specific. If you ask, "Will I ever become an actress?" the answer will be general and open because the question was too broad. Instead, try asking, "Should I try out for the school play?" or "Should I take acting lessons after school?" In this way you are dealing with the immediate situation. Questions that relate to a possible distant future are difficult because the future is always changing. Remember that Tarot cards won't predict your future — but they will illuminate your path.

Yes or no questions are okay — just keep in mind that cards won't provide yes or no answers.

Avoid questions that have two parts, like, "If I get a part-time job, will I be able to buy the boots I want?" The cards can handle only one question at a time. It might answer the one question — whether to get a job or if you'll get the boots — without acknowledging the other. Your reading will be too cluttered and it won't tell you what you want to know.

Try to keep a positive spin on your question. The cards work with your energy at the moment, so if you're full of anger or being negative, that will show up in your reading. Therefore, don't ask, "Why can't my Mom relax and stop giving me a hard time?" Instead, try, "What can I do to increase understanding between Mom and me?" It might sound corny, but your reading will be much more productive if you admit your responsibility in situations. You can't change your Mom's actions, but you can work on your reactions to them.

Be careful that you don't rely too much on the Tarot to handle the little things in life. If you find yourself asking if you should wear the blue or the green sweater, you know you've gone too far. The Tarot should be an extension of your daily life, not a controlling force.

Warning: There will be times when a reading just doesn't make sense — when the cards that you turn up don't seem to fit the question. Your first reaction might be to think that the cards are wrong, but don't give up so easily. Sometimes the Tarot answers things that we didn't even know we asked.

Step back and look at the reading without thinking about your question. Your subconscious may be trying to tell you that something else needs your focus. Are there a lot of Trump or Court cards? Is there a pattern of suits or themes? Give yourself some time to think about it. Record the layout in your journal to look at later. You'll find the answer if you look at it from different angles.

Keeping a Journal

This is one of the most important aspects in learning and enjoying the Tarot. A journal will start off as a place to record and analyze cards, but will quickly become an extension of the reading — a valuable tool in the Tarot experience.

Like most things with the Tarot, you will most likely change your journal process as time goes on and you know more about what you need. As things move from process to personal, you'll see a lot of changes. It's all about growth and discovery.

The purpose of the journal is to gather information, record data, and work out analysis.

You'll want to stop and think about the set-up of your journal. Important items to consider:

- ◆ Date of reading
- ◆ Type of spread
- ◆ Question asked
- ◆ Cards and their position
- ◆ What each position signifies
- ◆ The meaning of each card

Until you've had enough time to decide what will work best for you, try to include all of these points — and anything else you would like to add. Too much information is better than too little when you're starting out.

Ask yourself:

- ◆ What were my first impressions of the card?
- ◆ What images stand out?
- ◆ What are the characteristics of the suit?
- ◆ Is this a Destiny, Court, or numbered card?
- ◆ What are the other cards around it?
- ◆ How does it relate to my question?

You have a choice of analyzing your layout right away or saving it until later when you've had more time to process the information. (A good idea is to do a bit of both.) Write down whatever comes to mind:

- ◆ What is your overall impression of the layout?
- ◆ What challenges are facing you?
- ◆ Are there any cards that promise good fortune (like the Nine of Cups)?
- ◆ What should your next move be?

The wonderful thing about keeping this record is that you can return to older readings with a fresh outlook. Things often look different with a bit of distance and change in perspective. Has your analysis of these entries changed? Are you on the right path? Did you make the right decisions?

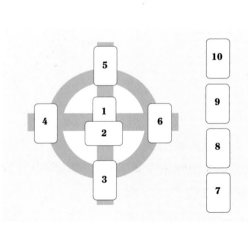

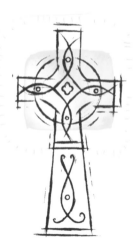

Here's an example of how your journal might look:

Celtic Cross Spread
(see also pages 81-82)

"How can I improve my study habits?"

Position 1 — *Significator:*

Position 2 — *Challenges in the present:*

Position 3 — *Past (what is passing):*

Position 4 — *Immediate past:*

Position 5 — *Future:*

Position 6 — *Immediate future:*

Position 7 — *You — your attitude and strengths:*

Position 8 — *Hopes:*

Position 9 — *Fears:*

Position 10 — *Outcome:*

My thoughts:

Thoughts at the end of the day:

Later additions:

Make sure that you leave yourself room to add something else later. You might not need it, but it never hurts to plan ahead.

Shuffling

The general rule is to continue shuffling until you're ready to stop. There won't be a specific sign — you'll just have to listen to your intuition to know when it's time to cut the deck and lay out the cards in the spread. Meditate on the cards, think about your question, and try to get rid of all the other thoughts running through your head. Shuffle the deck because the cards require your concentration. If you're reading for someone else, tell that person — the Querent — to shuffle the cards and concentrate, while you sit back and wait until she's finished.

You can mix up the cards any way you would like — the idea is spend some quality time with them before the reading. Follow the straight-ahead method of hand over hand, flip the cards into one another, whatever you would like. You could lay the cards face down on the table, create a big pool and move them around with both hands. This gives you the chance to see and touch them all before restacking and dealing them out. You'll have had a nice talk before getting down to business.

Cutting the Deck

When the shuffling is done, put the cards down in front of you and cut the deck using your left hand:

- Take a chunk of cards from the top and place it beside the remaining deck.
- Cut this second stack in two and place to the left of both piles.
- You now have three piles lined up.
- Restack them into a single pile — still using your left hand — in whatever order you would like. Do it quickly, without thinking too much about it.

The person who shuffles cuts the deck. If you are reading for someone else, that person would be the Querent. It is the Querent's energy that works with the cards. After the cut, take the deck back and place it in front of you.

You are now ready to start laying out the cards in your spread.

Laying Out the Cards

Look at all your options for Tarot spreads. Is there one that suits your particular question? Pick one that you like and lay out the cards according to its design. The first card is placed in Position 1, the second in Position 2, and so forth. (Assume that any spread design requires all the cards to be laid face up on the table before you begin.) Will you be reading cards in both the Reverse and Upright positions (see page 22)? If so, be cautious while turning them over from the deck. Turn them from side to side so that you will preserve the direction that they landed in the shuffle.

All at Once or One at a Time?

Sometimes it is best to see the cards all at once because you need to ponder the whole before pulling it apart. Other times, one at a time is most effective. Keep this in mind when you design your own spreads.

If any of the spreads in this book favor one method over the other, it will say so. Otherwise, do whichever feels most comfortable.

Reversed Readings

Unlike regular playing cards, Tarot cards have an Upright direction (or Divinatory) and a Reverse direction (basically, the picture is upside down). Some people read them differently. Not every Tarot reader agrees that a reversed reading of the cards is necessary. Some believe that all the information needed is found in the upright imagery — after all, there are cards that contain difficult messages — and reversed readings only complicate matters. Others argue that everything has its opposing force — and that can't be avoided. Isn't it better to know all the possibilities that lie before you? By the way, not all reversed readings are negative. Quite a few offer a positive spin on the situation.

You might want to use only upright readings when you're just starting out. It will keep things simple while you gain confidence with readings and layouts. It won't take you long to get comfortable. This is also something you could consider during those first times you're reading for someone else. If you don't feel comfortable adding the reversed position into the mix, then keep things light. The reading will be more productive if you don't feel stressed.

Setting the Mood

Create an environment that is comfortable, relaxing, and welcoming — a place where you would like to spend a lot of time.

What would work best for you? Music is a nice touch — although keep in mind that you want a comforting atmosphere, not a distracting one. If you're going to sing along with the lyrics and imagine yourself dancing with the lead singer, choose something else. If you don't have a room to yourself, block off an area to create some privacy. Try decorating it with pillows or pictures you like.

Wear something comfortable — track pants or pajamas. You might want to put on a special hat (your "Tarot hat") that you'll wear for each reading. Play a song or recite a chant or a blessing before you begin — something that will set the mood and let your mind know that it's time to start. Then relax and concentrate.

Focusing

One thing that often helps readers set their minds on the cards and interpret the questions is to recite a few words before shuffling. Find a poem, song, or prayer that relaxes you and brings the Tarot into focus — choose a few lines to deliver before each reading. This might become an essential part of the ritual, signaling you to set your concentration on the reading. Most people say aloud the same few lines each time, but you can vary this, if something else feels better. It could take you a while to find the words that work best for you. You might want to consider writing your own phrase. It will make the reading much more personal. It doesn't have to be anything elaborate or fancy — just a phrase that will help you concentrate and focus. What would you like to bring to the reading? Are you looking for insight or illumination? Would you like to thank someone before you start? Maybe you would like to draw attention to the world around you — nature, family, or friends. You could ask a question or simply state an intention. If a line from a favorite song feels especially poignant, choose that to open up your readings. As long as it helps you focus, you can't go wrong.

Put your left hand over the deck and say your few words out loud (you can whisper, if you'd prefer). Clear your mind as you speak — concentrate on the words and what they mean to you. If you are reading for someone else, pass the deck of cards to the Querent for shuffling when you're finished.

Take the Time to Learn and Understand

Have you heard the joke about the two guys in New York City? One stops the other and says, "Can you tell me how to get to Carnegie Hall?" The other answers, "Sure. Practice, practice, practice." The same is true of the Tarot.

The cards are fun and you will enjoy them whether you're a beginner or expert. But if you want to experience the Tarot as more than a party game — as something that will help you learn and grow — you'll need to put in some serious time. Pull your cards out every day, look at them, record your thoughts in your journal, explore the spreads, become comfortable with colors, designs, and ideas. Most important of all, enjoy your time with the cards. You'll be happy that you did.

THE MAJOR ARCANA

Appearances can be deceiving. It looks like the Tarot deck works in a straight line — from 0 to 21 — but don't let those numbers Fool you (pun intended). You'll be a lot better off if you think of the Tarot as a series of cycles — wheels working inside wheels — cogs in a machine. Life is in constant motion. Everyone's life is in constant motion (despite those feelings that "nothing exciting ever happens!"), and we are all affected by each other. We must pass through stages, one leading into the next as we learn and grow.

The Fool is innocence and the World experience. Follow the path from 0 to 21 — first we must learn about ourselves and our abilities as we develop relationships with others and move towards personal fulfillment. The Tarot helps illustrate the layers within us all — that we are all multifaceted. You can use the cards to clarify whatever question you ask.

0	The Fool
1	The Magician
2	The High Priestess
3	The Empress
4	The Emperor
5	The Hierophant
6	The Lovers
7	The Chariot
8	Strength
9	The Hermit
10	The Wheel of Fortune
11	Justice

12   The Hanged Man
13   Death
14   Temperance
15   The Devil
16   The Tower
17   The Star
18   The Moon
19   The Sun
20   Judgment
21   The World

These are the "destiny" cards — the Trumps. When a Trump card appears in your reading, you're being told about a topic you can't avoid — something that demands your attention. What did you ask the Tarot? What position does it have in the layout? Are you being told of a challenge that faces you or are you being reminded of support that you didn't realize was there?

Pay extra attention to cards from the Major Arcana. They are letting you know that something important is happening — something out of the ordinary. Perhaps it may seem to be something beyond your control — or it might require extra work. But, for sure, it's a sign that shouldn't pass by unnoticed.

THE FOOL.

THE FOOL   0

Although this sounds like an insult, it's not. This is where it all begins. This jaunty fellow doesn't seem to notice the severe drop in front of him and it's unlikely that he will care. He's travelling light — all his possessions fit into a tiny sack and he carries a single rose. This is all he needs to start his journey, nothing weighs him down and he's ready for his new adventure. The dog at his side indicates his connection to the animal world. His feet may be on the ground (for now) but he's looking towards the sky.

Divinatory

- The Fool is starting a new journey or adventure.
- One of the Fool's more prominent characteristics is innocence — a lack of experience that doesn't dampen his enthusiasm.
- Stepping into the unknown, trying something new, without fear of failure.
- You'll never know if you don't try.

Reverse

- You just can't take that first step.
- There has been a delay or setback in plans.
- Being a Fool — stepping blindly into the world — doesn't mean you can do whatever you want. Make sure that your actions aren't hurting anyone.

THE MAGICIAN   I

THE MAGICIAN.

The first step in making something happen. The Magician knows how to bring together all 4 elements — earth, air, water, fire — to turn an idea into reality. There are items from all four suits — a cup, pentacle, wand, and sword on the table in front of him. Above his head is the mathematical symbol for infinity. He holds a staff to the sky and points to the ground with his other hand. The Magician is using his natural abilities and here is the evidence that it works: flowers are blooming all around him.

Divinatory

- Turning an idea or dream into reality. Putting talents to work.
- You have plenty of plans and they all seem possible. You feel like you can accomplish anything you set your mind to.
- Natural abilities and personal strength are high.
- A good time to start new projects.

Reverse

- Not working at your full potential or ignoring your talents when they would be useful.
- Using your talents to take advantage of a person or a situation. Remember that you have a responsibility to others.
- An important opportunity slipped by without notice.

THE HIGH PRIESTESS.

THE HIGH PRIESTESS   II

Awoman sits on a throne bathed in blue light. There is a crescent moon on the floor before her, a full moon in her crown (symbols of spirituality). She is wearing a cross on her gown and is holding a half-hidden scroll that says TORA (symbols of organized religion). This is a wise woman. She has knowledge of the world around her, but her special wisdom concerns the inner self. She brings gifts of intuition and creativity.

Divinatory

- ◆ Let your intuition guide you. Sometimes logic doesn't have all the answers.
- ◆ There is mystery in this world — don't demand concrete answers all the time.
- ◆ If you feel you are stuck in the "same old place" and doing the "same old thing," try something new. Let go. See where your inner thoughts will take you.

Reverse

- ◆ Instincts are not providing good advice.
- ◆ You have become too superstitious and are being too cautious in your decisions.
- ◆ There may be some manipulation going on (by you or someone else).
- ◆ This is a time to step back before you make a decision. There may be more to the story than you see at the moment.

THE EMPRESS.

THE EMPRESS III

This is the classic Earth Mother card. She sits on a throne near a forest; her cloak is decorated with plants — nature is all around her. Have you noticed all the symbols of the female on her dress and throne? The Empress brings abundance, productivity, and a good crop (this doesn't have to be taken literally). Here is nature and nurturing at its best.

Divinatory
- ◆ You are in a very productive time and able to complete projects you start.
- ◆ You are enjoying a relaxed and comfortable environment where all your basic needs are met.
- ◆ Enjoy the rewards, the fruits of your labor, the bounty of the harvest — you get the idea.

Reverse
- ◆ The promised bounty isn't coming.
- ◆ There may be troubles at home.
- ◆ New ideas just aren't coming and you feel like you've hit a creative roadblock.

THE EMPEROR.

THE EMPEROR   IV

White hair and beard, throne, crown, armor, staff — there's no denying this is a King, a ruler. This man is in charge and he knows it — carries an Egyptian ankh in one hand (spirit and immortality) and a globe (control of world around him) in the other. This is a leader, an authority figure, who uses logic to solve problems and assist others.

Just because it is a man sitting in this throne, don't assume that it is only a man who can hold all this power. (This is true of all the cards in the Tarot deck.) These were traits most commonly associated with men when the cards were created. An awful lot has changed in the past century!

Divinatory
- This is someone in a position of power or authority, someone who might have the answers you are looking for.
- Logic, clear thinking and rational thought are needed.
- It's time to remember that everyone is responsible for his or her own actions.

Reverse
- The person in a position of power isn't using authority responsibly.
- The decisions being made are not wise or careful.
- Be careful that your emotions aren't too strong — which makes it difficult to make decisions.

THE HIEROPHANT.

THE HIEROPHANT   V

This card is also known as the Pope. There is a lot of imagery on this card that indicates the Catholic Church — the staff he is carrying, the crossed keys at the bottom, and the two priests he is blessing. These symbols might be important to you or they might not. The important thing is what they represent. Hierophant means "revealer of secret things" and symbolizes conventional wisdom and learning. The card speaks of the greater good of the community, not personal gain.

Divinatory

- ◆ A school or religious institution — a place of learning.
- ◆ A teacher or educator.
- ◆ A time to choose the conventional path.
- ◆ Sometimes it's best not to rock the boat or cause a scene. Sometimes it's best to work with a group to achieve something great.

Reverse

- ◆ There is a challenge to authority and making your own decisions.
- ◆ Finding your own path in non-traditional ways — learning doesn't only come from textbooks.
- ◆ Possibly a hasty decision made for personal gain.

THE LOVERS.

THE LOVERS   VI

This card is not only about romance, though that plays a part. It deals with all relationships; the give and take needed to achieve a good balance; the different parts that make up a whole; commitment and responsibility. The male represents the conscious mind and the female represents the unconscious mind. He looks to her and she looks towards the Angel Raphael who seems to be passing on information. This card is about love and partnership, but also understanding yourself and others.

Divinatory
- Friendships are important to you.
- You need to find balance and harmony.
- Make sure you know all the details before making a choice.

Reverse
- A friendship isn't balanced or is having difficulties.
- You don't know what you want.
- Advice from others is only confusing you more.

THE CHARIOT.

THE CHARIOT   VII

What would you need to drive a team of charging horses (or according to this design, Egyptian sphinxes)? Control. You need to harness the forces around you to keep steady and on track. It requires stamina and focus. The sphinxes that lead this chariot are black and white, male and female, symbolizing opposite or opposing natures in this world. When they work together, the driver can follow his chosen path.

Divinatory

- ◆ Success will come with hard work and effort.
- ◆ You are focused and intent on achieving your goals.
- ◆ A person who is responsible and concerned.

Reverse

- ◆ There is a loss of control and focus.
- ◆ Difficulty finishing tasks or projects.

STRENGTH   VIII

STRENGTH.

There are two kinds of strength — physical and spiritual — and you need both to reach harmony. Someone would have to be pretty brave to get that close to a lion, pet it and touch its mouth. This woman has overcome her fears — pushed them aside and tamed the wild beast. Sounds like a fairy tale, doesn't it? Well, that probably isn't a coincidence.

Divinatory

- ◆ Face your fears head on — it's the only way you will overcome them.
- ◆ Look inside yourself for strength.
- ◆ Don't let your emotions take control.

Reverse

- ◆ Don't abuse your power or play dirty.
- ◆ You need to control your emotions.

THE HERMIT.

THE HERMIT   IX

There's something to be said for a personal retreat. This card doesn't necessarily stand for the "wise old man in the woods," but it does suggest that you choose your own path. Meditate on that single light to attain your goal. Take the time to step back and reflect. And what does all this quiet contemplation bring you? Sound and wise advice (from yourself or others, depending on where this card turns up in your spread).

Divinatory

- ◆ You know what is best for you.
- ◆ The Hermit offers the promise of sound advice coming your way.
- ◆ Don't rush into your next project. Instead, take time to sit and think things through.

Reverse

- ◆ Good advice has been ignored.
- ◆ You haven't learned from past experiences.
- ◆ You are lost in thoughts and daydreams.

WHEEL of FORTUNE.

THE WHEEL OF FORTUNE   X

Despite its name, this card is not about game shows or spinning letters. It appears in the middle of the Trump cards to remind us of the cycle of life, time without end, and that all things pass. Life is filled with ups and downs and there's little we can do about it. This card has a lot to do with luck and karma, but you're not without grounding. At each corner of the card a sign of the zodiac (clockwise from top left: Aquarius, Scorpio, Leo, Taurus) reminds us there is some stability.

Divinatory

- ◆ You're having a string of good luck — you're on a roll.
- ◆ The timing is right.
- ◆ Things are looking up.

Reverse

- ◆ You've hit a snag and things are slowing down.
- ◆ Try not to worry too much. Relax and let these difficult times pass.
- ◆ There's been an unexpected turn of events.

JUSTICE.

JUSTICE   XI

This card looks almost barren compared to others that are filled with flowers, mountains and signs of the zodiac. This woman is straightforward, honest and fair — weighing the pros and cons in life and balancing them out. Life isn't always easy but it will work out in the end. Ask yourself, "What is fair?" and "What do I deserve?"

Divinatory

- ◆ You need to keep yourself open to others so you can see all sides.
- ◆ There might be hard lessons to learn.
- ◆ The right thing will happen in the end.

Reverse

- ◆ A decision has been made that is unpleasant or unfair.
- ◆ There is a lack of balance.
- ◆ Someone is giving you unwise advice.

THE HANGED MAN   **XII**

You might want to start by asking yourself how he got himself into this predicament. More than likely he didn't choose to be caught in the snare or hang upside down from a tree. The fact is, though, he's there and doesn't seem to mind it so much. This is a card about letting go and finding a new perspective on life. Maybe you've found this new outlook by choice, or perhaps circumstances have led you to it. It doesn't really matter. The important thing is that you enjoy the view — and learn from it.

Divinatory
- ◆ A new outlook on life.
- ◆ You might have to sacrifice or lose something to gain new perspective.
- ◆ What is important in your life? Focus on the things that matter.

Reverse
- ◆ You are stuck doing the same old things and you've fallen into a rut.
- ◆ Sometimes the only way you can move forward is to let something else go — and this is a sacrifice that you may have to make.
- ◆ You are having difficulty making decisions.

DEATH.

DEATH   XIII

This card isn't about death in the physical sense, despite what you might think. A skeleton returns from battle leaving waste and destruction in his wake. That's the left side of the card, behind him. On the right are people welcoming his arrival. There is gold, flowers, and the rising sun. It's about transformation, the changing of the seasons, renewal and rebirth — telling you it's time to move on. Leave the old ways behind and start something new.

Divinatory

- ◆ Changes are occurring in your life.
- ◆ After a period when your life has felt stagnant, there is renewal. A new burst of energy.
- ◆ New ideas and creativity when starting projects.

Reverse

- ◆ That much-needed change hasn't taken place yet. Things are at a standstill.
- ◆ You might be putting things off.

TEMPERANCE.

TEMPERANCE   XIV

Temperance is often connected with moderation but that tells only half the story. It is about self-discipline, evening out excesses, and finding a middle ground for two opposing forces. Balance is always important. It allows us to see clearly where we've been and where we're going. The archangel Michael stands with one foot on land and the other on water. He is pouring water from one chalice to another, balancing conscious and unconscious, emotions and logic.

Divinatory

- ◆ You have a great deal of patience when dealing with others or trying situations.
- ◆ Seek harmony and balance.
- ◆ Learn to relax and take things as they come.

Reverse

- ◆ You are impatient when dealing with others or trying situations.
- ◆ You are feeling stagnant and unable to finish projects.
- ◆ You aren't learning from previous experiences. You are repeating the same mistakes.
- ◆ Learn to slow down.

THE DEVIL.

THE DEVIL   XV

Two figures — male and female — are chained to a block that has a devil perched on top. Notice, though, that the chains are loose and escape is possible. The humans have the power but must act on their own. This card is a warning that you are too wrapped up in — or obsessed with — something. This is an unhealthy situation. Ask yourself if there is something (or someone) who has taken too much control in your life. What can you do to change this circumstance?

Divinatory
- ◆ You are stuck in a situation that isn't making you happy. You need a change.
- ◆ You are too attached to material things and ignoring your spiritual side.
- ◆ You are being too forceful in a situation or when dealing with someone. It might be time to relax.

Reverse
- ◆ You've been released from the situation that was making you unhappy.
- ◆ Past experiences have taught you well and you've faced the fears that were holding you back.

THE TOWER.

THE TOWER   XVI

Needless to say, the people depicted in this card weren't expecting this sudden bolt of lightning. There is fire, storm, and falling from a great height to an unknown fate.

This is not about just any old change — it is something unexpected, out of the blue, and it will affect you in important and vital ways. It is a force that shatters your tower. Now it's time to start over and rebuild.

Divinatory

- ◆ An unexpected change.
- ◆ Deal with it and move on.

Reverse

- ◆ This doesn't necessarily mean that you've avoided the "sudden change" of the Divinatory Meaning. It might be mean that it will arrive but will be less drastic or powerful.
- ◆ There's something that you're avoiding.

THE STAR.

THE STAR XVII

Have you ever wished upon a star— and had it come true? This requires faith — belief that your wish will be heard — trusting that when you put something "out there," it will come back to you. Once again a figure has one foot on land and the other on water. Rather than pouring water from one chalice to another, she is pouring it on the land and the pond — sharing it, returning it to its source. Don't lose sight of your hopes and dreams. You have the power to reach your goals. There is strength and courage in your imaginings.

Divinatory
- This is a time when anything is possible.
- Your hopes and dreams just might come true.

Reverse
- There has been a loss of faith.
- Your dreams seem unattainable.
- You might be suffering from a lack of confidence in your intuition and low self-esteem.

THE MOON.

THE MOON XVIII

The Moon looks down on a world divided. A road cuts the card in two. On one side is a dog representing the domestic, civilized world and on the other is a wolf from the animal, untamed world — both are baying at the Moon. This card reminds us of our dual nature and that things aren't always what they seem. Moonlight can be deceptive and things may remain in the shadows. Your imagination is working full force, which may be good but may not. What are the other cards saying? Take a closer look.

Divinatory
- ◆ Disagreements and emotional outbursts.
- ◆ It's not a good time to make important decisions.
- ◆ Your imagination might be working overtime.
- ◆ There might be something in your unconscious that needs to be expressed.

Reverse
- ◆ Things might not be perfectly clear, but you aren't lost in confusion.
- ◆ Your imagination is no longer working overtime. You can trust your instincts again.
- ◆ Making decisions is less difficult because things seem more clear to you now.

THE SUN   XIX

THE SUN.

It's a bright sunshiny day! Time to rejoice and celebrate. A young child sits on the horse. The four sunflowers on the wall behind her represent the four suits of the Tarot, the four compass directions, and the four elements that guide us all. The world is restored and the future is bright.

Divinatory
- Satisfaction, happiness, and success.
- Enjoy this time when everything feels wonderful.

Reverse
- You are reminded that the sun doesn't shine every day.
- You are still stuck in the past and unhappy memories.
- You lack the necessary faith in yourself to find happiness.

JUDGMENT   XX

he Archangel Gabriel is blowing his horn, calling everyone to attention — it's a wake-up call
for your spirit. Transformation is nearly complete.
You've passed the tests, proven your abilities and
strength, but you're not done yet. Clarity is needed
to see the new world, new personal powers, and
awareness. You're nearing the finish line, so don't
lose faith or sight of your goals.

JUDGEMENT.

Divinatory

- ◆ You know that you're close to reaching
  your goal and it's renewed your energy.
- ◆ Personal awareness is heightened.
- ◆ Just when you thought you knew everything .... there's something more.

Reverse

- ◆ You're dragging your feet about taking that final step.
- ◆ You are ignoring your spiritual side, and that creates an imbalance.
- ◆ Are you clinging to a dream or fantasy that's unrealistic?
- ◆ Avoid superstitions.

THE WORLD XXI

The cycle is complete! You've done a great job of meeting challenges and overcoming obstacles. You've opened yourself up to new ideas and situations. There are some similarities between this card and the Wheel of Fortune — a circle held in place by the four points at each corner. This time around, though, a woman dances at the center of the wreath, celebrating her success. Look back on where you've been and what you've accomplished and give yourself a pat on the back. Congratulations! Now it's time to move on to the next cycle.

THE WORLD.

Divinatory
- ◆ You've earned this success.
- ◆ Share your riches and experience with others.
- ◆ You've found what you were looking for.

Reverse
- ◆ More concentration is required. Remember that anything worthwhile takes time.
- ◆ Don't give up — you're so close.
- ◆ Low self-esteem may be slowing you down.

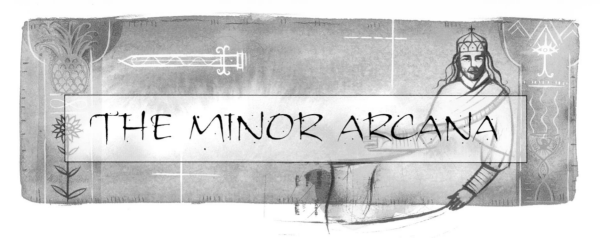

THE MINOR ARCANA

The Minor Arcana are "free will" cards. They deal with the daily events of life. While they will reveal aspects — both positive and negative — that affect you, you still have the power to react. You can direct them by your actions. If you don't like what they say, alter the energy. If you are warned that you aren't trusting your instincts enough, it is up to you to learn to do so.

Each suit in the Minor Arcana — there are four — Wands, Cups, Swords, and Pentacles — follows a cycle from 1 to 10. Important signposts along the way are:

♦ The Ace (number value of 1) is all about new beginnings. All the power and energy of the suit (Cups deal with emotion and love, Swords with intellect and truth) appear full force in the Ace.

♦ The Fives represent an important turning point. This is the moment when things start to break down.

♦ Tens are about crossing the finish line. They usually indicate success on most fronts, but be careful. The journey isn't over yet. Have a good look at everything you've carried across the line — make sure that you aren't weighing yourself down.

♦ The Court cards tell the same story as the numbered suit cards — moving from innocence to experience — but with human characters. They are the personification of the suit's qualities. Some people believe that each court member represents a person of a specific age and gender: the King is an older man — a father figure, the Knight is a reckless young man and so on. Don't let these stereotypes influence you. Any one of us may be capable of offering wise advice like the king, or committing an impetuous act, like the reckless knight.

♦ Pages are enthusiastic and thoughtful — often quiet and contemplative.

♦ You will notice that all the Knights are on horses. Horses represent action and movement. Knights are energetic and on a quest.

◆ Queens represent balanced, mature individuals with thoughtful insight. They are often caring and nurturing.

◆ Kings in each suit offer experience and authority. They will provide good advice. They don't let their emotions get the best of them in any situation.

The Four Elements

According to ancient philosophy and wisdom, four elements — or essential forces — make up the balanced whole of the earth: Earth, Air, Water, and Fire. Each person is made up of these four elements, as well, although we generally have a tendency to focus on one more than the others.

In the Tarot, each element is associated with one of the suits in the Minor Arcana and is a guiding force.

Fire	Wands
Water	Cups
Air	Swords
Earth	Pentacles

It will help you, as you learn about the Tarot, to remember that each suit contains the properties of the element.

Fire — By understanding and controlling this element we have moved forward as a civilization — heat, technology, fuel to cook with and light our way. It can help or harm us. It is never still, but always active and moving. Fire can also represent the sun, its strength, and its power over the earth.

Water — It cleanses, purifies, sustains, and comforts us. Our bodies and the earth are made up of mostly water. It symbolizes vision and wisdom — our spiritual and intuitive side. The waters of life flow from cup to cup. A cup contains the water that instills emotion and spirituality in our lives.

Air — Something that we can't live without and we certainly can't avoid. It is everywhere — surrounding and pervading us — it nourishes our bodies. We have found ways to use its energy — harnessing the wind to power many kinds of machines — but we know that we can touch only a small portion of it.

Earth — Our primary home, it provides all the resources we need and teaches us lessons in balance and harmony. This is the material base of our lives — grounded and (it is to be hoped) secure.

WANDS

Energy, enthusiasm, and drive characterize this suit. Notice that the Wands throughout their cycle are multitasking. Each card is used for something different — support, defense, shelter, and more. This is because Wands have the ability to make things happen. Through communication and endeavor, ideas become reality. Wands have the fire and passion to get things done.

Ace of Wands

ACE of WANDS.

All the Aces have the same look. A hand extends seemingly from nowhere. One large wand with all its power is before you: enterprising, ambitious, and hard working.

Upright
- New beginnings, a great start, creation, invention.
- Abundance of ambition and motivation.

Reverse
- Lack of motivation, worn out.
- Decadence, something essential is missing.
- Time to start again at the beginning — regroup.

Two of Wands

A man is waiting — standing on a castle wall, holding a globe and looking out over land and sea. Riches and fulfillment are on their way.

Upright
- Waiting, patient, helpful.
- Possible suffering involved, disappointment, sadness.
- Fortune, things will begin to happen.

Reverse
- Lack of movement, balance, or harmony.
- Element of surprise and wonder.
- Frustrations and delay.

Three of Wands

A man looks off into the distance, this time with his back to us. He is looking towards the future and watching as his ships come in. Investment and enterprise is paying off.

Upright

- ◆ Cooperation, support, establishment.
- ◆ Reap the benefits from hard work.
- ◆ Increase in momentum and discovery.

Reverse

- ◆ Despite all your hard work, you just aren't making any progress.
- ◆ Too much activity prevents clear sight.
- ◆ An end to troubles and disappointments.

Four of Wands

The four wands act as posts for a canopy while two people celebrate beneath. The garden is blooming, everyone is happy, because all your hard work has paid off.

Upright

- ◆ Celebration, attainment of ideals.
- ◆ Harvest, garden, fruition.
- ◆ Refuge, peace, harmony.

Reverse

- ◆ Still a positive card, but things aren't as grand.
- ◆ It's the little things that mean the most.
- ◆ Appreciate the people and bounty that surround you.

Five of Wands

Conflicts arise. Five men clash with their wands. They aren't divided into teams but are fighting each other. If these opposing forces would put down their wands and stop fighting long enough to see all sides, they might clear up the issue.

Upright
- ◆ Confusion and conflict.
- ◆ Need to clear things up before acting, in need of advice.
- ◆ Take a good look at your surroundings.

Reverse
- ◆ A break in the fog.
- ◆ Make the most of a bad situation.
- ◆ Litigation, disputes.

Six of Wands

More than a celebration, this is someone returning victorious, receiving recognition after a battle is won. The rider wears a laurel wreath and there is another on his wand. There may be a homecoming or a successful journey on its way.

Upright
- ◆ End of a difficult time, good news.
- ◆ Things will soon improve.
- ◆ A safe journey.

Reverse
- ◆ Frustrated, just can't make something work.
- ◆ There are some delays but try not to get too stressed about them.

Seven of Wands

This young man is holding his ground, defending his piece of land. There is competition; it might be one against many, but there is strength and you have the advantage.

Upright
- Things are tough but you'll make it.
- Strength, perseverance, success.

Reverse
- You've reached the end of a difficult time and are stronger for it.
- Progress is slow but steady.
- Time of indecision. Be careful.

Eight of Wands

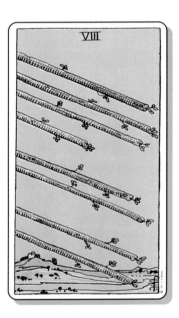

It's not quite clear sailing but pretty close. There is flight, movement, and momentum in the right direction. Something new is starting and you're on your way to reaching your goal.

Upright
- Things are moving; success is around the corner.
- You are flying high.
- A time of hope.

Reverse
- Journey postponed.
- Be careful of out-of-control feelings. Keep them in check.
- Don't make rash decisions. Watch before you speak or leap.

Nine of Wands

The bandage tells us that this fellow has been injured, but he's prepared for the next attack. He's learned from past experiences. There have been some struggles, but you've made it this far and a solution is near. Strength of character and stamina will take you far.

Upright
- Learn from past experiences.
- Know how to defend yourself, friends, or family. You aren't afraid of competition or opposition.
- You are prepared for whatever may come your way.

Reverse
- Lacking in stamina, not finishing what you started.
- Obstacles are before you and you're not prepared, too vulnerable.
- Are you worried about something? Disappointed?

Ten of Wands

His arms are full; he looks like he's about to tip over, and there is still a while to travel before he can rest. He's taken on too much. Work will suffer when sloppily done.

Upright
- Something is weighing you down.
- Too many responsibilities and you can't please everyone.
- Oppression from an outside force.

Reverse
- Releasing yourself from extra burdens.
- Opposing forces are at work.
- Time to take responsibility for what is yours and get the job done.

Page of Wands

This Page brings good news. He doesn't take new information lightly. He thinks things through and can be relied upon to tell the truth.

Upright
- ◆ Good news.
- ◆ Young or immature, still dependent on others, adventurous.
- ◆ Faithful, vibrant character.

Reverse
- ◆ Delay in plans.
- ◆ Unwanted news or delayed messages.
- ◆ Can't make decisions.

PAGE of WANDS.

Knight of Wands

As is always the case with the Knight card, this person is ready for action. A horse charges forward, the Knight firmly holding the reins. You might think he's chaotic or messy, but that is because he doesn't waste time and gets right to the task at hand.

Upright
- ◆ Hasty, quick reactions.
- ◆ Enthusiastic, jumping right to it.
- ◆ Departures, flight, changes in life.

Reverse
- ◆ Things are disorganized.
- ◆ Break or fracture, discord.
- ◆ Enthusiastic energy is reversed.
- ◆ Personal conflicts on the rise.

KNIGHT of WANDS.

Queen of Wands

A black cat sits before a woman on a throne — both are keen observers and quick. She holds a single sunflower, which reminds us of strength, growth, and potential. This is a strong woman, welcoming, friendly, enthusiastic, and motivated.

QUEEN of WANDS.

Upright
- Strong, ambitious, business-minded.
- Outgoing, possibly aggressive.
- Honorable, respectable, agreeable, loving.
- Creating new paths and directions.

Reverse
- Overly aggressive, overly passionate.
- Possible infidelity.
- Economical, practical.

King of Wands

This King is looking away, but he provides space for approach. He is kind and wise, an authority figure who doesn't allow power to go to his head. He always wants to offer help and advice. Enthusiastic and motivated, he wants the best for everyone.

KING of WANDS.

Upright
- Enthusiastic about life and people, passionate, honest.
- Always has advice, wants to help, encourages others, positive outlook.
- Believes anything is possible.

Reverse
- Pessimism and doubt have the upper hand, insecurity, uncertainty.
- Good person but stern, serious yet charitable.

CUPS

The Cup holds the waters of life. It contains our emotions, creativity, and all matters that we associate with the heart. This suit focuses on topics like love, relationships, imagination, friendships, and celebration. Cups can bring much joy or a great deal of sorrow, because it is our emotions that they affect.

Ace of Cups

Aces hold the entire potential of the suit. Emotions and heart are opening up — ready to send and receive. Start of a new journey in love and spirituality.

ACE of CUPS.

Upright
- Heart opening up to new love, wonderful beginnings.
- Nourishment, fertility, abundance, good health.
- Awakening spirituality, rising consciousness.

Reverse
- Insecurity about a new relationship, not open to new love or starting over.
- Things are changing, unstable, not what they seem.
- Unfortunately, you don't always get what you want, and you must learn to deal with this.

Two of Cups

Two friends are pledging their loyalty and commitment to each other by sharing cups. This card indicates a balanced and cooperative relationship.

Upright
- Balance, sharing, harmony, opening up to someone.
- Commitment, union, friendship.
- Good news on its way.

Reverse
- Imbalance in relationship, or within yourself (too emotional? too passionate?).
- Reached an impasse and someone has to make the first move.
- Is it time to step back? Or to sever ties and move on?

Three of Cups

There's a party going on around here. After much hard work you've succeeded, and now it's time to celebrate. Three women dance in a field of flowers and bounty, with cups held high. They are feeling joyful and festive.

Upright
- Time to celebrate and enjoy! You've worked long and hard and it shows!
- Happy endings, victory, healing.
- Possible talents in the arts.

Reverse
- Celebrations might be getting out of hand. Too much excess, overindulgence.
- It's possible that someone has been hurt by your excesses.
- Time to get things back under control.

Four of Cups

A young man sits below a tree, lost in thought. His crossed arms and legs, and bent head, tell us he is not open to the new cup coming his way. He has removed himself from society and is lost in his own troubles.

Upright
- Detached, separated from others, emotionally distant.
- Lots of inner turmoil.
- Feeling misunderstood, tired of communication.

Reverse
- Ready to return to society after solitude.
- Starting new projects or relationships.

Five of Cups

Three cups have fallen and spilt their contents. This man feels a loss (and since Cups deal with emotions — this has been an emotional loss) and his sadness is all-consuming. If only he would turn around to see the two full cups behind him. Strength to overcome the situation is there, but he needs to acknowledge it.

Upright

- ◆ Loss, grief, bitterness.
- ◆ Wallowing in self-pity or loss.
- ◆ Keeping things locked up inside.

Reverse

- ◆ Turn that frown upside down!
- ◆ Rising above ideas of loss or unhappy events and moving on.
- ◆ Kinship, new alliances.

Six of Cups

A boy gives a cup filled with flowers to a girl in a town courtyard. This is meant to illustrate happy times in the past or someone that you haven't seen in a while.

Upright

- ◆ Something or someone from your past returns.
- ◆ The past holds happy memories, brings good tidings.

Reverse

- ◆ Time to let go and move on, time for renewal.
- ◆ Unhappy memories.

Seven of Cups

Seven cups float before a man — each filled with something wonderful, something that he desires. He can't make a decision because too many choices are open to him. He is lost in dreams and imagination.

Upright

- ◆ Imagination has kicked into high gear and is clouding your decisions.
- ◆ Lost in dreams, missing the important details.
- ◆ Some progress.

Reverse

- ◆ At last a decision has been made.
- ◆ Determined to meet goals, on the right track.

Eight of Cups

It is night. A man walks away, leaving on a journey. He is in need of a retreat. Eight gold cups are stacked at the front of the card, representing something he once desired but which no longer makes him happy. Time for a drastic change.

Upright

- ◆ Unhappy with present situation, desires change.
- ◆ Realizing something is not as important as you thought.
- ◆ Focus on inner thoughts, spirituality.

Reverse

- ◆ Rejoice, feast, return to material world.
- ◆ After a personal or spiritual retreat, you have returned to the rest of the world. You feel rested and secure.

Nine of Cups

This is a fine card and one that you'll want to find in any wish spread. A man sits before a wall of cups, looking very pleased with himself. Success and happiness in whatever you wish.

Upright

- ◆ The "wish card."
- ◆ Success, security, victory.

Reverse

- ◆ Imperfections, anxiety.
- ◆ Having to wait for the desired outcome.

Ten of Cups

Ten cups form a rainbow with a family rejoicing below. You've reached your goals. Whatever you wished for has come true.

Upright

- ◆ Your dreams will come true.
- ◆ Everything is working like a dream.
- ◆ Perfection.

Reverse

- ◆ Home life is unsatisfactory, causing pain among loved ones.
- ◆ Delays in reaching a satisfying conclusion.

Page of Cups

Once again, the Page brings us news. This time around it's a message of romance or help from family and friends. His presence is a sign that things are changing for the better.

PAGE of CUPS.

Upright
- ◆ A young man, gentle, creative, possibly providing assistance.
- ◆ Approaching joy, happiness, something good in your life.
- ◆ Things are changing for the better.

Reverse
- ◆ Moods and emotions are strong and need to be kept in check.
- ◆ Prefers solitude, doesn't express feelings or needs.

Knight of Cups

He is not racing through the countryside but moving calmly, holding the cup before him. This Knight is creative and artistic — and also thoughtful and intelligent.

KNIGHT of CUPS.

Upright
- ◆ A romantic dreamer. A young man with his head in the clouds.
- ◆ The beginning of something new — a romance?
- ◆ An open heart, open to new ideas and people.

Reverse
- ◆ A fraud, dishonest, probably hiding something.
- ◆ There isn't an emotional balance in the relationship.
- ◆ Doesn't play well with others.

Queen of Cups

She sits on her throne surrounded by water, and we know that water represents our emotions and spiritual nature. It is intuition, rather than logic, that rules her world. Her concerns lie with the well-being of others. She wants everyone to be healthy, happy, and comfortable.

QUEEN of CUPS.

Upright
- ◆ A fair, honest woman.
- ◆ Devoted, caring, artistic.
- ◆ Intuitive and emotional.

Reverse
- ◆ Full of exaggeration, overactive imagination.
- ◆ Means well but can't be trusted.
- ◆ Actions require more than intuition alone. Stop and think.

King of Cups

The waters surrounding his throne are turbulent and chaotic but he is calm and reserved. He keeps his cool during the storm. Compassion guides him — and will assist you, as well.

KING of CUPS.

Upright
- ◆ Thoughtful and fair.
- ◆ Emotional, artistic, concerned.
- ◆ Creative intelligence.
- ◆ Calm personality.

Reverse
- ◆ Dishonest, possibly deceitful.
- ◆ Emotions too strong, difficult to handle.
- ◆ Detached, lack of perspective.

SWORDS

Mental clarity and intellect — like a sword slicing through the air — guide this suit. The power of the mind through communication and ideas will combat any obstacle. But a sword can cause harm and conflict, as well. Watch which way it is pointing. This suit is full of action — be careful that it isn't destructive action.

Ace of Swords

A crown with laurels sits atop the sword. You will succeed in a new project, but action is necessary. A sword is sharp, focused, and direct; it will cut through any difficulties.

ACE of SWORDS.

Upright
- ◆ Starting a new successful venture.
- ◆ Heightened emotions.
- ◆ Powerful, triumphant, in control.

Reverse
- ◆ Slow down, take it easy, you'll catch more flies with honey than with vinegar. A new project will have troubles.

Two of Swords

A woman sits blindfolded with her back to the water and moon (two sources of intuition and feelings). She is locked into place while balancing two swords. She needs to make a decision, a decisive move, but is at a complete loss. She needs to remove her mask and look around.

Upright
- ◆ Have lost sight of goals.
- ◆ Reached a stalemate, feel stuck.
- ◆ In need of advice and guidance.

Reverse
- ◆ Need to make a decision and get moving.
- ◆ Be cautious of advice and surroundings.

Three of Swords

Three swords pierce a heart surrounded by rain clouds and a storm. Pain, sorrow, loss — something that will make a heart ache — is nearby or on its way.

Upright

- ◆ Remorse, sorrow, loss, absence.
- ◆ Arguments.

Reverse

- ◆ Emotionally removed, dissatisfied.
- ◆ Things are starting to turn around and will be fixed soon.

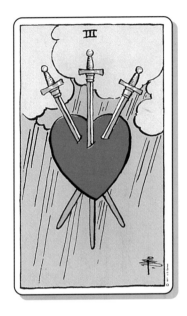

Four of Swords

This is a Knight at rest (not dead, as some people think at first) after a long struggle. It appears that he's in a church, which suggests a spiritual retreat. He needs to think and reboot.

Upright

- ◆ Retreat, repose, understanding.
- ◆ Not struggling against obstacles but accepting their presence.

Reverse

- ◆ A lot is happening, both positive and negative.
- ◆ Think things through before acting.
- ◆ Wise advice at work.

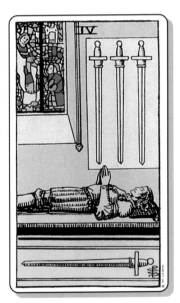

Five of Swords

You'll have to decide what took place before this picture. We see a smiling, triumphant man in possession of all five swords while two other men walk away in defeat or sorrow. Was there a fight among them? Are they preparing to do battle elsewhere? Either way, you can see that they aren't all getting along and that the first man is not concerned or sensitive to their troubles. There has been a break in their relationship due to one person's actions.

Upright

- ◆ Selfish actions, manipulation, destruction.
- ◆ Abuse of power, degradation.

Reverse

- ◆ Reaching some even ground.
- ◆ Trying to pick a fight.
- ◆ Some success but much less than anticipated.

Six of Swords

The woman and child in this boat are obviously troubled and sad, but they are moving to a happier place. Notice that the waters on the right of the boat are stormy, while the water on the left (the direction they are heading) is calm. Things have been tough, but they are looking up.

Upright

- ◆ The end of a difficult time, balance restored.
- ◆ Beginning a new journey.
- ◆ Setting your sights on new goals and a bright future.

Reverse

- ◆ Can't get past a bad situation.
- ◆ Need to rethink plans and attitude.
- ◆ Confession, declaration.

Seven of Swords

Who owns the swords that this man is stealing? The other cards in the spread will help you find the answer. It requires planning and confidence to pull off this maneuver. But it might also indicate deceit and someone being tricked.

Upright

- ◆ Plans, design, action.
- ◆ Confidence.
- ◆ Deception, beware of the plans of others (look at the other cards to know their intentions).
- ◆ You aren't being told the whole truth.

Reverse

- ◆ Instruction, good counsel.
- ◆ Truth revealed.

Eight of Swords

All right, this woman's situation does not look good. She's blindfolded, tied up, surrounded by swords, and standing in a muddy puddle. It's understandable that she's frightened. This card is about our fears and how these fears control our lives. There are many swords around her, but they are stuck in the ground — they don't threaten her — and she could easily move through them to safety — if only her fears weren't holding her in place.

Upright

- ◆ Bad news, fear, indecision.
- ◆ Afraid of letting go.
- ◆ Sickness.

Reverse

- ◆ Decisions made, optimism returns.
- ◆ Finally free.
- ◆ Still some difficulties.

Nine of Swords

This woman is suffering a great deal. She has had a terrible loss and isn't coping with it very well. She is in need of comfort and advice — something to help her sleep through the night.

Upright

- ◆ Time of strife, unrest, uncertainty.
- ◆ Delays, deception, loss of hope.

Reverse

- ◆ Doubt, suspicion, fear.
- ◆ Time of healing.
- ◆ The end is in sight.

Ten of Swords

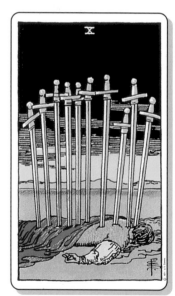

Ouch! You need to remember that the numbered cards depict an idea — not an actual event. This indicates a sudden or violent end to a cycle. You know that you've reached the end because there is no place else to go. Look at the man in the picture — there is no mistaking that he has reached his finish.

Upright

- ◆ Division, divorce, final result of turmoil.
- ◆ Sense of loss and completion.
- ◆ End of the line.

Reverse

- ◆ Impermanence, detached from past pain.
- ◆ A new cycle will begin soon. Hope for the future.

Page of Swords

His sword is upright and ready to do battle. He is intelligent, vigilant, and inquisitive. Since swords are associated with intellect and mental clarity, the Page is telling you to take notice of things around you. Ask questions and examine things closely.

PAGE of SWORDS.

Upright

- ◆ Lightning-fast reflexes, on the ball, quick-witted.
- ◆ Curious, inquisitive, "spying."
- ◆ Courage may be needed.

Reverse

- ◆ Revelation is coming.
- ◆ Unpredictable, unexpected events might turn out for the best.
- ◆ Communication brings truth.

Knight of Swords

This is a man on a mission. His horse is racing and his sword is aloft. This is a time for action. When this card appears in your spread, it could mean a person or event coming into your life. It will be something important that requires immediate attention. Don't waste time in dealing with it.

KNIGHT of SWORDS.

Upright

- ◆ Something is about to happen. Keep your eyes and ears peeled.
- ◆ Brave, quick to respond (although possibly in anger).
- ◆ Ready for anything.

Reverse

- ◆ Conflicts and delays.
- ◆ Incapacitated, mentally worn out, picking a fight.

Queen of Swords

As she sits on her throne, we see more blue sky and clouds than earth. Intellect and mental clarity are her main concerns. The Queen holds her sword steady with one hand while gesturing with the other. She is open and welcoming to people, rarely becomes too emotional, and offers good, sound advice.

QUEEN of SWORDS.

Upright
- Reserved, thoughtful. Quick intelligence.
- Adaptable, capable, and observant.
- Possible sadness or mourning.

Reverse
- Suffering a loss.
- Closed off, prejudiced, driven by pride, judgmental.
- Just waiting to explode.

King of Swords

His throne is a lot smaller than the other Kings', — and he is not as concerned with material goods and earthly delights. He's a thinker, a logical, well-informed leader. Notice how he stares right back at the reader? This is a man who watches people, observes them closely, and understands.

KING of SWORDS.

Upright
- Educated, understanding of intellect, good logical advice.
- Associated with authority and power.
- Knows how to get to the heart of the matter, direct, forthright.

Reverse
- Worn out after too many obstacles.
- Overly critical, cruel intentions.
- Having difficulty dealing with bad news.

PENTACLES

This suit is also known as Coins or Disks. It is grounded in the material things of life — finances, resources, possessions, and work. Pentacles focus on security and wealth or the lack of ability to maintain them.

Ace of Pentacles

All the powers of the Pentacles suit — material goods, money, finances — are associated with this card. It represents the physical rather than the spiritual side of life.

ACE of PENTACLES.

Upright
- A wonderful card!
- Prosperity, happiness, success in new ventures.
- Money or gifts coming soon.

Reverse
- Greed, obsessed with money and material gain.
- Not using your talents for good purposes.
- The bottom might be about to drop out.

Two of Pentacles

Quite literally, this is about juggling finances and projects. The sea is wavy behind this fellow, but he's concentrating on the two Pentacles. His plan seems to be working.

Upright
- Need to find a balance.
- Good advice or message on its way.

Reverse
- False gaiety, putting on a brave face (but not fooling anyone).
- Time to reorganize and prioritize.

Three of Pentacles

A stonemason is finishing work at a church and is waiting to be paid. It's hard work carving stone and he deserves the acknowledgement. Soon people will notice all of your hard work — recognition is on its way. This may be money or praise or a heartfelt thank you.

Upright
- ◆ Hard work and acknowledgement.
- ◆ Time to pat yourself on the back.

Reverse
- ◆ Delay in receiving your due.
- ◆ Mediocre work performance.
- ◆ Disagreements.

Four of Pentacles

This man is very attached to his pentacles and seems unlikely to let go. He doesn't have to worry about money or material goods because there is a solid foundation (his feet are firmly planted on two coins) to support him. He has worked hard and is proud of his accomplishments.

Upright
- ◆ Overly attached to material wealth.
- ◆ Work hard to attain and keep possessions.
- ◆ Not generous with money, very cautious.
- ◆ Not worried about finances.

Reverse
- ◆ Watch your finances — it might be the right time for a budget.
- ◆ Losing firm grounding. Be cautious.

Five of Pentacles

These two are outside in the cold, struggling through the snow. They are impoverished. The question is, "What kind of loss have they suffered?" Is it personal or spiritual? Have they lost money or something precious? The situation and spread may need a closer look.

Upright
- Difficulty with personal foundation — whether spiritual or financial.
- Need to pay attention to health issues.

Reverse
- Change of luck, return of hope.
- Accept and understand that life offers good and bad.

Six of Pentacles

The scales are balanced and money is being distributed fairly. This card represents the sharing of wealth or a bonus or gift arriving soon. It is not certain which is the central character of the card — the man standing or the two receiving his gifts. You might identify with either. And remember that "what goes around, comes around." If you give now you might receive later. It's all a part of the balancing act.

Upright
- Gratification, satisfaction in unions and commitments.
- Sharing rewards.

Reverse
- Jealousy, unfairness.
- Rewards might not come free of charge.

Seven of Pentacles

A man with a garden hoe gazes at a bush filled with pentacles. He has tended this plant and it has blossomed. He is not surrounded by wealth and riches but has succeeded in set goals. There is satisfaction in solid accomplishments.

Upright
- ◆ Time to collect rewards and profits.
- ◆ Investments will pay off with solid accomplishment.

Reverse
- ◆ A poor return on investments, or smaller than expected.
- ◆ Anxious about finances.

Eight of Pentacles

He is focused on the task at hand, producing one disk after another. A dedicated worker who puts that little bit extra into a project.

Upright
- ◆ Success at work.
- ◆ Well rounded, focused.
- ◆ Preparing yourself for the next stage, the new direction.

Reverse
- ◆ Trouble at work/school or with finances.
- ◆ Ambition has slowed down.
- ◆ Not using talents to full potential or for something dishonest.

Nine of Pentacles

This is a woman who has it all. She looks very content and at peace with herself. A garden in full bloom, a bird perched on her arm, she is surrounded by nature in all its glory. There is more than enough to share with others.

Upright

- Secure, independent, generous.
- Know when to slow down and enjoy things.
- Feel connected to people and world around you.

Reverse

- Fear, anxiety over money or business.
- Incomplete or abandoned projects.
- Lack of trust, too dependent on others.

Ten of Pentacles

While the Nine of Pentacles depicts the abundance of nature, this card tells us of the riches of the material world. Three generations of a family celebrate inside a city's walls. They have riches, security, and each other.

Upright

- Balance of finances and family life.
- Security and comfort.

Reverse

- Poor choices in finances or gambling.
- Loss of money.
- Family insecure.

Page of Pentacles

The message says that luck in the material world is on its way. Our messenger boy is confident, inquisitive, and studious. He is enthusiastic about his work and always puts in that extra effort.

Upright
- ◆ A scholar, practical, ambitious.
- ◆ Good luck in the material world.

Reverse
- ◆ Unfavorable news, bad news about finances.
- ◆ Wants material gain but not willing to work for it.
- ◆ Lazy.

PAGE of PENTACLES.

Knight of Pentacles

Despite the presence of a horse on this card, there is no movement. He is watching and waiting for the right moment. When the time is right he will leap into action. He is compassionate, thoughtful, and laid back.

Upright
- ◆ Trustworthy, responsible, helpful.
- ◆ Good with finances.

Reverse
- ◆ Unable to focus, careless, neglectful of duties.
- ◆ Irresponsible, doesn't finish projects.

KNIGHT of PENTACLES.

Queen of Pentacles

We are back in nature. The land is fertile and full of color. This Queen makes sure that everyone is well taken care of, safe and secure. She is generous with her wealth and talents.

QUEEN of PENTACLES.

Upright

- ◆ Fertility, abundance, generosity.
- ◆ Hard worker, responsible, caring.
- ◆ Likes to take care of people.

Reverse

- ◆ Suspicious, moody, insecure.
- ◆ Afraid of failing, so rarely tries.
- ◆ Needy, mistrustful.

King of Pentacles

It's hard to tell where this King's robes end and the vines and plants begin. He is not merely surrounded by wealth and abundance; he is a part of it. With his eyes closed and hands gently holding a disk and scepter, he looks easy-going and approachable. Kings are always full of advice and good thoughts — this one is here to help with answers to money matters and to advise about issues that require logic and clear, analytical thinking.

KING of PENTACLES.

Upright

- ◆ Generous, intelligent, good with finances.
- ◆ Logical, thoughtful, brave.
- ◆ Steady and true.

Reverse

- ◆ Sneaky, corrupt, lazy, bad with finances.
- ◆ Thinks things should just be handed to him.
- ◆ Interested only in material gain.

THE SPREADS

t's time to put all that picture-learning into practice — the Tarot in action! This is how we communicate with the Tarot: We ask a question, then shuffle and cut the deck. Then we lay out the cards in a particular pattern called a spread, placing each card in a specific spot (a position) that has a particular significance unique to each spread. The meanings of the cards in their positions relate to the question you asked while shuffling the cards.

The Meanings of the Cards

How are you going to learn the meanings of all those cards? Well, you don't have to know them at the start, but one of the first things to do when learning the Tarot is to become comfortable with the cards and relate them to your life. You will notice that some cards stand out for you from the start. Others will take a while to get to know. This is natural and very much like meeting new people. It might seem like a daunting task at first, but time flies when you're having fun.

Don't worry if you have to look up meanings of cards even after you consider yourself a seasoned reader. This isn't a test. Sometimes readings are confusing. Keep in mind that you're asking questions in order to learn about the unknown, which means that the unexpected might show up. It's hard to know every possible interpretation — keep your options open and don't be afraid to ask for help. That's why we have books like this.

Let's look at the Map of the World layout. This spread uses the four directions of a compass to give an overall view of your situation. You have asked the Tarot, "How can I communicate better with my sister?" Shuffle and cut the deck and then lay down the cards — by choosing the first one on the top of the pile. Start with Position 1, and begin your reading. Look up the meaning of each card (upright or reversed) and consider how it relates to the position of the spread.

Map of the World

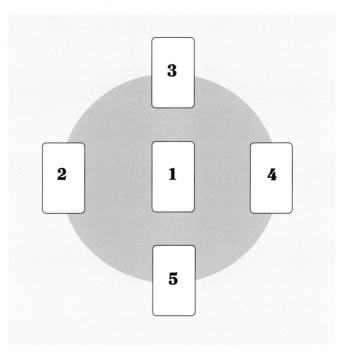

Position 1 — *Significator* — Where you stand. Represents you at the moment of the reading and what you feel about the subject.

Position 2 — *West* — The past. What has happened in the past — usually recently — concerning the subject.

Position 3 — *North* — Your unconscious mind. Something hidden inside you that you've yet to recognize that relates to the question asked.

Position 4 — *South* — Your conscious mind. What you are bringing to the situation — the opinion you hold about the question.

Position 5 — *East* — The future. What the immediate future has in store for you. Often these future cards represent a challenge that you must overcome.

There are several sections in this book with different layouts in them. Don't feel limited to using these spreads only for the occasions that the book suggests. If you choose to use one from the Birthdays section, for example, when it isn't anyone's birthday, that's perfectly fine.

Celtic Cross

The Celtic Cross, which you've already seen on page 18, is a traditional Tarot spread — one that has been used for years — and Waite's is the standard version. It covers the aspects of life — past, future, hopes, fears, what supports you, what you must overcome — with specific cards allowing you to examine the details. You can spend a great deal of time with this spread.

The spread on the next page is the original version of the Celtic Cross, as shown in *The Pictorial Key to the Tarot* by A.E. Waite. For this one, the Querent (you or the person you're reading for) chooses the Significator — a card that you feel best represents you. Put this card in Position 1. Shuffle and cut the deck. Draw another card ("what covers her") and place it on top of the Significator. Place the next 9 cards as the map on page 82 indicates.

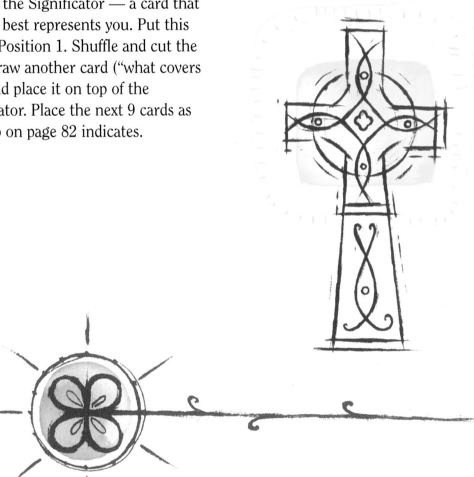

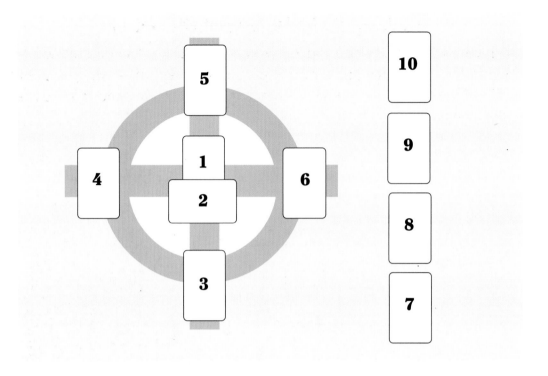

Position 1 — *Significator.*

Position 1 — *What covers her.*

Position 2 — *What crosses her.*

Position 3 — *What crowns her.*

Position 4 — *What is beneath her.*

Position 5 — *What is behind her.*

Position 6 — *What is before her.*

Position 7 — *Herself.*

Position 8 — *Her house.*

Position 9 — *Her hopes and fears.*

Position 10 — *What will come.*

Getting to the Bottom of the Matter

This spread is useful when you know what you need to focus on but want more information. By looking into the roots of the question — why you need to ask it in the first place — you will receive additional insight about how to meet your challenge.

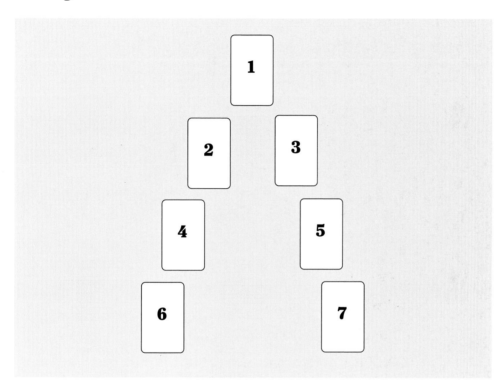

Position 1 — *Represents the question.*

Position 2 — *What you want.*

Position 3 — *What you need to focus on.*

Position 4 — *Lessons from the past.*

Position 5 — *Advice from others.*

Position 6 — *Your fear.*

Position 7 — *Your hope.*

The Tools for Success

This spread will tell you what you need to do to get the job done right, the things you need to work on. These are the tasks that you need to focus on. It follows the pattern of a pentagram with the Outcome card as the center.

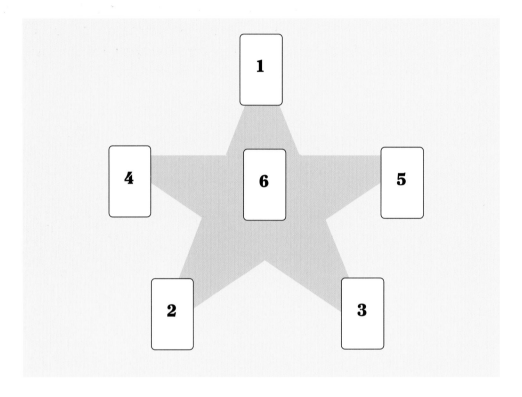

Position 1 — *Significator.*

Position 2 — *What will aid you.*

Position 3 — *How others will help you*

Position 4 — *What you need to leave behind.*

Position 5 — *What you should include.*

Position 6 — *Outcome.*

A Time for Action

You know that you have to do something. It's time to take that first step toward your goal. What will you encounter along the way? How will it all turn out?

Don't put the cards out all at once — take your time. Lay the cards out in pairs (Positions 1 and 2, Positions 3 and 4, Position 5). Reading two cards together provides additional information at each stage. Pause before you turn over the next pair so you have the chance to let the information sink in. You don't want to rush important decisions.

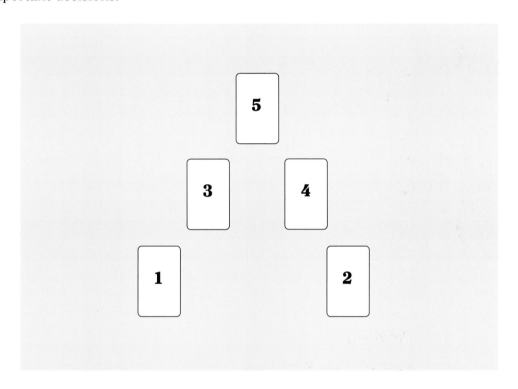

Positions 1 and 2 — *Represents the question.*

Positions 3 and 4 — *What you will encounter when you take action.*

Position 5 — *Outcome.*

Both Sides of the Problem

Sometimes, no matter how close we are to people, things don't always work smoothly. We fight, we argue, there are misunderstandings. Maybe it's because we are so close — spend so much time together and are so important to each other — that we fight with a person we love. It's often our families who hold this special place (or our best friend in the world). If you have any siblings, you will know this feeling only too well. This layout will help you deal with these situations. When there is a disagreement, ask the Tarot to show you what led to it and how you can prevent it from happening again.

Position 1 — *What surrounds the question.*

Position 2 — *What went wrong?*

Position 3 — *What needs to be done?*

Position 4 — *What to watch for.*

Position 5 — *Outcome.*

Loves Me, Loves Me Not

What are the chances that the person you're sweet on likes you back?

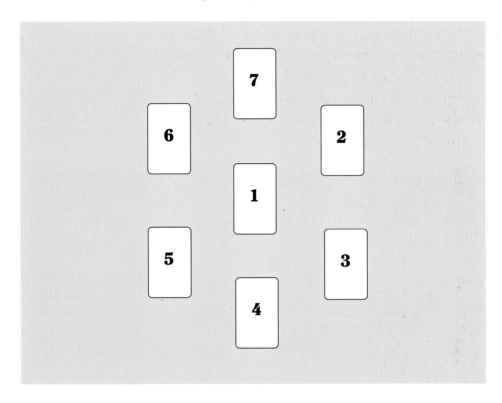

Position 1 — *How you feel at the time of the question — your attitude towards your crush.*

Position 2 — *How do you see the object of your affection?*

Position 3 — *What mistakes from the past should you learn from?*

Position 4 — *How do the two of you connect?*

Position 5 — *Where do you divide?*

Position 6 — *What kind of action is needed?*

Position 7 — *Outcome.*

How Can I Improve my Self-Esteem?

Lay down cards 1 through 4. When you reach Position 3 during the reading, if the answer is "yes," flip over the next card in the deck. Even though it is listed as Position 5, read it before you hit Position 4. The reason for this is that not everyone, or every reading, will require the fifth card.

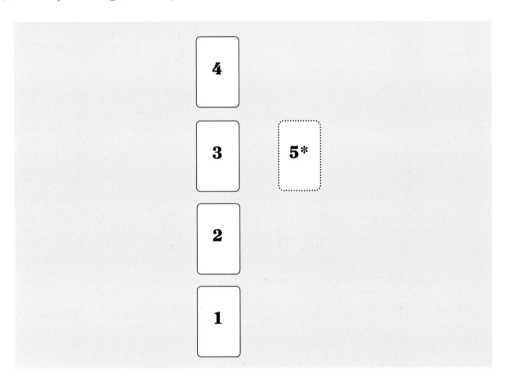

Position 1 — *What do you see when you look in the mirror?*

Position 2 — *How do you think others see you?*

Position 3 — *Do I need a change of attitude? (*If yes, turn over Position 5 and read it.)*

Position 4 — *Am I being honest with myself?*

Position 5 — *What should I do?*

Starting a New Project

For any time you're starting something new — whatever it may be.

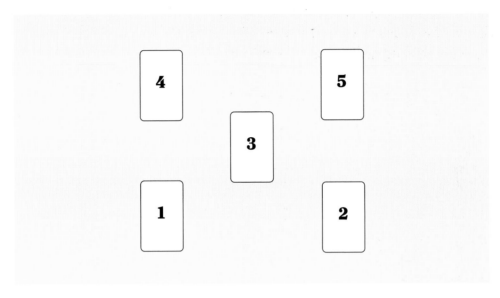

Position 1 — *What are you looking for?*

Position 2 — *What you will find.*

Position 3 — *What others expect.*

Position 4 — *What you already know.*

Position 5 — *What you'll need to know.*

Am I Ready?

It's not easy knowing when it's time to start going out with someone. It's not just about the two of you liking each other — you have to be ready. If you step into something too soon, you may be faced with dissatisfaction.

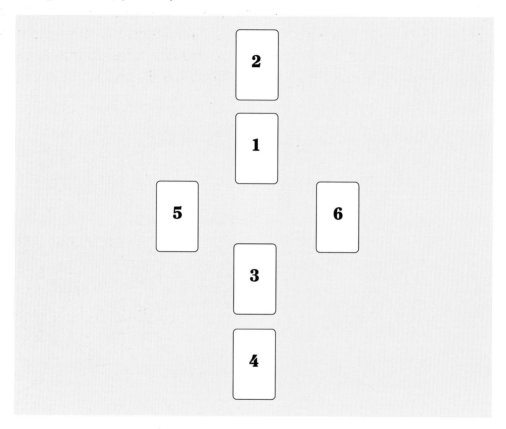

Position 1 — *How you see yourself.*

Position 2 — *What you will bring to a partnership.*

Position 3 — *What you need to overcome.*

Position 4 — *Warning card or sign of good things to come. (Reading depends on this card — what it signifies)*

Position 5 — *What is really important to you.*

Position 6 — *Outcome.*

The Power of Two

This spread is used when two people need to work through a problem. It will work if you are one of the Querents or if you are reading for others. Querents should take turns shuffling the cards while concentrating on the issue at hand. One cuts the deck and the other restacks it. Querents fan out the cards in front of them facedown. Querent A picks a card first and places it in Position 1. Querent B chooses a card and places it in Position 2. The two Querents take turns picking cards. Querent A chooses 1, 3, 5, 7, and 9. Querent B has 2, 4, 6, 8, and 10.

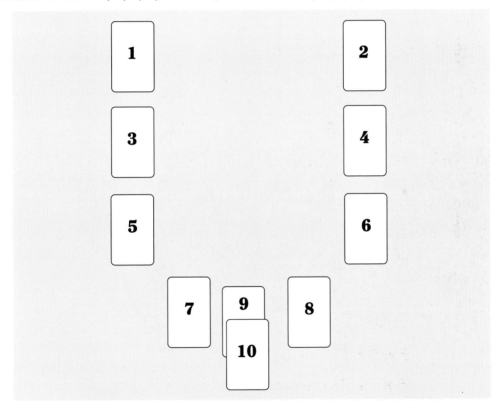

Positions 1 and 2 — *What you see with regard to the question.*
Positions 3 and 4 — *What you want.*
Positions 5 and 6 — *What you need.*
Positions 7 and 8 — *What you need to do.*
Positions 9 and 10 — *The combined energy of the Querents*
(Place 10 on top of 9)

This layout shows the two sides of a situation. Wait until all the cards are turned over and you've each had a chance to consider their interpretations, and let the information sink in. Then discuss what you see and how it relates to your situation. Start with what each of you recognizes (Positions 1 and 2), talk it through honestly, listening to what the other person has to say. Work your way through to the combined energy cards (Positions 9 and 10). Be just as open to your friend's interpretations of the cards as you are to your own.

A Bird's-Eye View

This layout works especially well with new friends or acquaintances because it has a simple design. It is a 7-card spread that gives an overall analysis of the question. It looks at it from different sides before providing the outcome card. Although you read the cards from Position 1 through 7, you need to see them as a whole. They are all working at the same time with regard to the question.

When reading for someone you don't know, many people choose to keep things as light and positive as possible. Ask the Querent not to ask a question that is overly serious or that might provide an unwanted answer. Keep all the cards in the upright position.

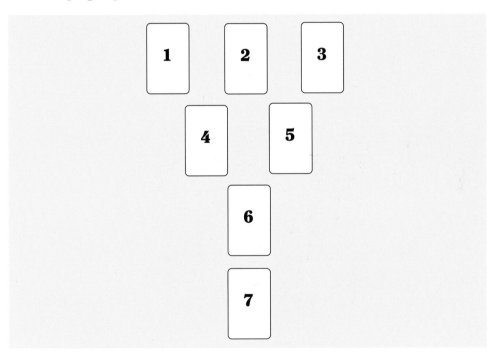

Position 1 — *What is surrounding the question.*
Position 2 — *Either the Querent or thoughts surrounding the question.*
Position 3 — *What the Querent hopes will happen.*
Position 4 — *What will occur.*
Position 5 — *Opposing forces.*
Position 6 — *Something the Querent doesn't expect.*
Position 7 — *Final outcome.*

Celtic Cross II

Because you can never have too much of a good thing!

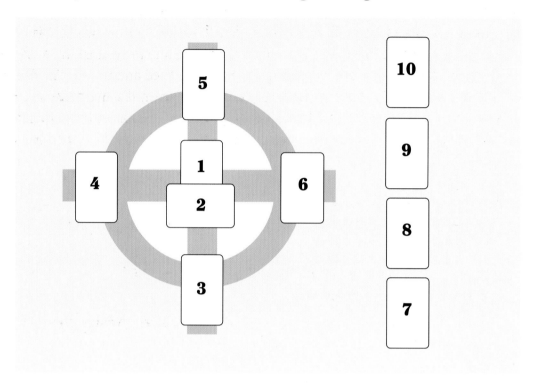

Position 1 — *Significator.*

Position 2 — *Challenges in the present.*

Position 3 — *Past (what is passing).*

Position 4 — *Immediate past.*

Position 5 — *Future.*

Position 6 — *Immediate future.*

Position 7 — *You — your attitude and strengths.*

Position 8 — *Hopes.*

Position 9 — *Fears.*

Position 10 — *Outcome.*

Design Your Own Spreads

As time goes on you'll probably have one or two subjects that you focus on more than others. Whether it's school or friends or trying to decide what you might want as a career, you will more than likely have a layout or two that is most effective. It's likely that this system is working out just fine for you. Many of these spreads have been around for a very long time and are tried and tested. They've been answering people's concerns for many a year. However, it's also possible that you have a nagging question that keeps popping up, and no matter how efficient your favorite spread is, it seems to be missing something. Maybe it's time for you to design your own spread.

Ask yourself a few questions:
- ◆ Are you looking for something that is generic or centered on a specific topic?
- ◆ Are the opinions of others important to the question?
- ◆ Do you need to examine the past?
- ◆ Are you concerned with the immediate past/future as well as the long term?
- ◆ Is an outcome card needed?
- ◆ Which card should come first?
- ◆ Should your layout have a specific shape?
- ◆ Do you have to read the past before you can know the present — or even the future?

Design a few prototypes and try them out a few times. If they don't provide a very good response, modify them until they do. You might find that your readings will have an extra bit of insight. But don't get into a rut and rely solely on spreads of your own making. Spice things up every once in a while — try different layouts — new ones, old favorites, something that someone else has created. Try as many different paths as you like.

Reading for Someone Else

Reading for yourself is very different from reading for someone else. All the principles are the same — shuffling and cutting the cards — following the layout pattern for the spread — but you can't read them like your own. Let the Querent (the person asking the question) know the possible interpretations of each card and how they relate to one another in the spread. Try not to draw conclusions — that's for the Querent to do — you are there to offer possibilities. It's sometimes difficult to read someone else's cards and not see only what you want to find. How difficult it is depends on how well you know the Querent. Is she a close friend? Someone that you've just met? A friend of a friend or an acquaintance? No matter how well you know a person, you don't know everything. And the cards might be telling her something that even she doesn't realize. Read the cards as you see them, as they unfold. Consider their title and design, their position, suit, whether they're upright or reversed. Tell the story that you see before you without making assumptions about the question or what the Querent should hear. You don't have the answers either — you're just the messenger passing on valuable information.

When reading for someone else, it's best not to know the question. It might skew your judgment, especially if Querent is a close friend. You might already have an opinion. At the end, if the Querent wants, you can look at the spread again with the question revealed.

Try to limit table talk. The Querent, of course, can speak, make comments, or ask questions. As a Reader, you will have to explain each card and its significance. The danger is that too much talk might sway the reading. Take your information from the cards — talk shop later.

There are times when a card you turn over will have negative connotations. How will you handle this situation? You will need to put a positive spin on it. If the Five of Cups appears, mention that the Querent may perceive a loss and feel sad, but note that there are two full cups promising opportunities. If the Nine of

Swords appears, look at the cards surrounding it. Do they reveal anything positive? What position does the card hold? If the Querent must face the Nine of Swords in her future, call attention to the fact that this is a "free will" card. She has the power to change her circumstances. Review the reading and look for ways she could choose to alter her path.

It is up to you to make the Querent's reading as beneficial and hopeful as possible. The truth sometimes hurts, but difficulties always open the door to opportunity.

Asking Questions about Someone Who Isn't There

You can do readings for someone else without having them with you. It's more difficult — and you should probably wait until you've had a lot of practice and experience — but it can be done. The hard part is separating yourself from the person in the reading.

If you are close to the person, or you are asking a question that is somehow connected with yourself, it is highly likely that you will show up in the reading. In fact, this is something that you should always be careful about, no matter how accomplished you become. Try to stay focused and ask yourself (honestly! Don't worry, no one will hear your answer — this is just between you and the cards!) if you have a personal stake in the question or its outcome. If the answer is yes, wait until you have more distance.

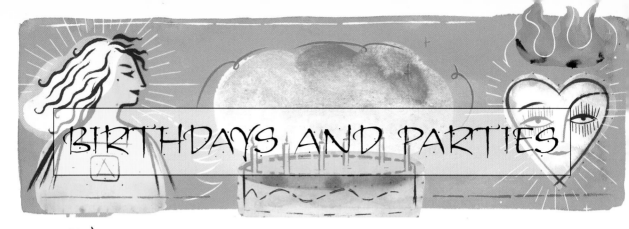

BIRTHDAYS AND PARTIES

These spreads fall into two categories. The first contains layouts that are especially appropriate for special occasions like birthdays. The other has spreads that are easy to do in groups and that don't take too much time. If you are planning to do readings for each of the partygoers (or even a few), you will want a layout that isn't too complicated. It makes for a poor reading if you feel rushed.

Don't do your readings in the middle of the group with everyone else watching. Find a private place for you and the Querent to sit. Make sure you're comfortable and there aren't too many distractions. A secluded corner or another room will work best.

Birthday Cards

Find your birthday Trump card by adding all the digits of your birthday. Keep adding the numbers together until you reach a result that lies between 1 and 22.

For example: if you were born on December 10, 1988

+1+2+1+0 +1+9+8+8 = 30

3+0 = 3

Your personality card is 3 — **The Empress**

    1   Magician

    2   High Priestess

    3   Empress

4	Emperor
5	Hierophant
6	Lovers
7	Chariot
8	Strength
9	Hermit
10	Wheel of Fortune
11	Justice
12	Hanged Man
13	Death
14	Temperance
15	Devil
16	Tower
17	Star
18	Moon
19	Sun
20	Judgment
21	World
22	Fool

Note that the Fool has the number value of 22. We couldn't leave the Fool out since there are so many people who are Fools (and we mean that in the best possible sense)! Therefore, it has the next available number after 21, the World. This makes sense when you think about the cycles of the Tarot. As soon as we finish one we start the next one at the beginning — back to being the Fool.

Read through the Major Arcana section to discover the interpretations of your personality card. How well does it describe you?

Calendar Layout

This layout isn't only for birthdays. It's perfect for all special events — anniversaries, graduations, holidays — especially New Year's Eve.

If this is a birthday reading, Position 1 should be the next calendar month after the birthday. So, if the birthday is March 8, 1990, then Position 1 should be April. Each position will let you know about important details to watch for in the year to come. It doesn't answer a specific question but gives a general reading of the events and challenges coming your way, based on the person you are on the date of the reading.

Will this be a precise reading? For instance, if the Tower card appears in the October position, does that mean you'll experience a sudden change in that month? Most likely it won't be that exact, but it will provide a good overview of things to come. Remember, too, that life is always in motion, and as you heed the earlier warning and good omen cards that appear, events later in the year will be affected.

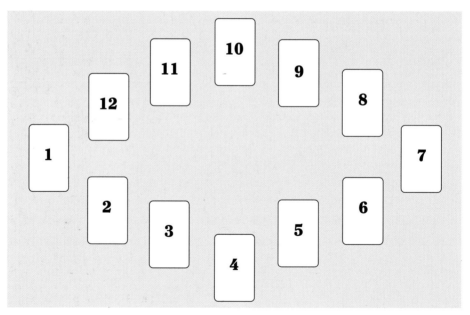

Otherwise:

Position 1 — January   **Position 5** — May   **Position 9** — September

Position 2 — February   **Position 6** — June   **Position 10** — October

Position 3 — March   **Position 7** — July   **Position 11** — November

Position 4 — April   **Position 8** — August   **Position 12** — December

What the Year Will Bring

The number of cards in this spread depends upon the age of the Querent (although 18 is the maximum you should use). This is why it's so good for birthdays.

It starts off like every other reading. The Querent shuffles and cuts the deck while clearing her mind of everything but questions of what the year will bring. The next step is to fan the cards out facedown. She needs to pick the number of cards that correspond to her age (12 cards if she's 12, 15 if she's 15, etc.).

The Reader takes these cards and lays them out. The layout differs slightly with each year but there is a basic shape to follow.

- ◆ There are always 5 rows.
- ◆ The first and last rows have only one card each.
- ◆ The middle three rows resemble an upside down triangle.
- ◆ The 2nd row always has more than the 4th.

Example 1: 18 years old

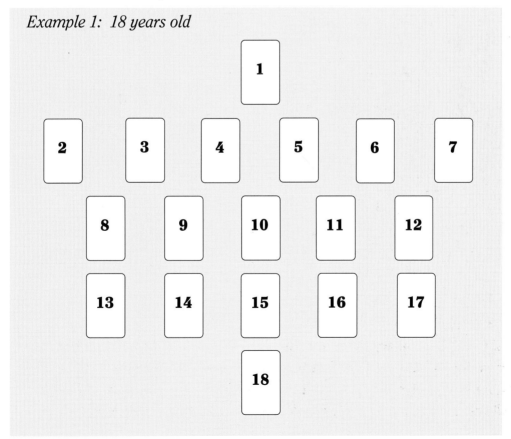

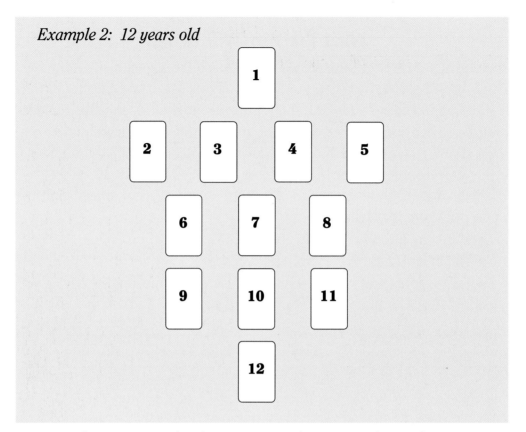

Example 2: 12 years old

Here is a chart to remember how many cards are in each row for ages 10 to 18.

Row #	10 yrs	11 yrs	12 yrs	13 yrs	14 yrs	15 yrs	16 yrs	17 yrs	18 yrs
1	1	1	1	1	1	1	1	1	1
2	3	4	4	4	5	5	5	6	6
3	3	3	3	4	4	4	5	5	5
4	2	2	3	3	3	4	4	4	5
5	1	1	1	1	1	1	1	1	1

What each row signifies:

Row #1 — *The Querent at the time of reading.*

Row #2 — *What you bring to the reading — past experiences and knowledge.*

Row #3 — *What will aid you throughout the year to come.*

Row #4 — *Obstacles or challenges you may face.*

Row #5 — *Outcome — final result — where you will be at your next birthday.*

Wish Spread

Make a wish. Ask if it will come true.

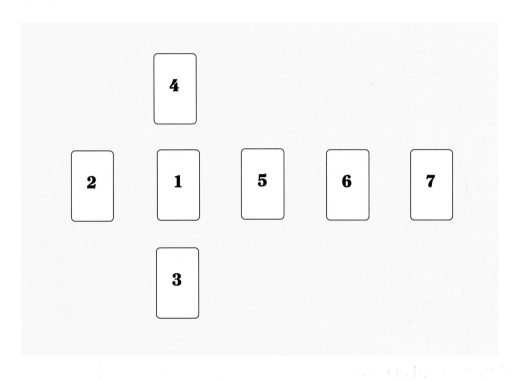

Position 1 — *Present state of mind.*

Position 2 — *What will help make your wish come true?*

Position 3 — *What are you afraid of?*

Position 4 — *How can others help?*

Position 5 — *What must you let go of?*

Position 6 — *What will you learn along the way?*

Position 7 — *Will your wish come true?*

The Story behind the Question

Smaller layouts can be just as effective as larger ones, but they provide a lot less detail. Sometimes it's good to get right to the heart of the matter. This spread examines the wish itself rather than giving you a yes or no answer.

Position 1 — *What I really want.*

Position 2 — *What I really need.*

The next three spreads are not technically Tarot layouts. They will not provide insight into your psyche or personal understanding. However, you will learn more about the cards themselves and have the opportunity to put your imagination to work.

Storytelling with the Tarot

This is a good way to get to know the cards and their various interpretations. It won't provide insight or clarification to your questions. In fact, you're not using the Tarot for its intended purpose. You're using the cards to tell a story — the meanings of each card determine the next step in the story — which will help you see their various sides and interpretations.

Since this isn't a genuine Tarot reading, you don't need to follow the standard procedure. There's no need to shuffle in the usual manner, cut the deck, or say your opening prompt. You aren't asking a question so there is no need for pre-reading concentration.

The first thing to do is separate the Court cards — that's the Page, Knight, Queen, and King — from the rest of the deck. We'll call the rest of the cards the Action deck. Shuffle each pile separately and leave them side by side.

You can lay the cards out one at a time (if you want the element of surprise) or all at once (if you like to see all the pieces before you begin your tale).

This is a game that you can play with friends. Each can pick a card and tell a portion of the story.

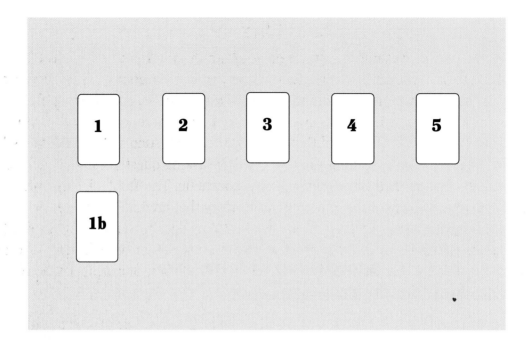

Position 1 — Choose this one from the Court cards that you've already piled separately. This is the main character in your story. If you would like to start with more than one person, pick another Court card and place it below Position 1 (we'll call this Position 1b). Use the characteristics of that card to create the character.

Position 2 — What is happening at the beginning of the story? Choose a card from the Action deck. The card will describe an action or obstacle — someone waiting, a new project, or a celebration. Invent a situation that suits this card.

Position 3 — What happens to the characters that sets the story in motion? Choose another Action card. What is happening in it? Is this something that your main characters chose to do or something that happened to them?

Position 4 — Choose another card from the Court card pile. A new person comes into the story. Who is it? How does he or she affect the story?

Position 5 — From the Action pile — what happens to bring about the climax of the story?

Tarot Characters

So, you've done readings for yourself, your family and friends. Maybe you've even tried to give your cat or dog a turn at the cards. It's been fun, you've enjoyed yourself, and discovered things along the way. Now, its time to get back to the books — put all that energy back into studying. If only there were a way to combine your two loves — Tarot and English class. Fear not, such a layout does exist!

Not a genuine Tarot reading, since you will be asking questions about fictional characters, but you might be surprised what comes up. The Tarot will uncover those bits of information and ideas about the story that are hiding just below the surface. Why can't Hamlet get his act together? Why does it take so long for King Lear to see the truth? Pick the character of your choice — male or female — from any story you'd like and ask the Tarot to reveal them to you. Remember that all answers relate to the character, not you.

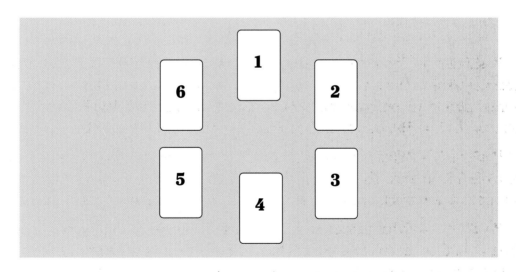

Position 1 — *What is the character's motivation?*

Position 2 — *What is her downfall (tragic or otherwise)?*

Position 3 — *What is her greatest asset?*

Position 4 — *What is her greatest challenge?*

Position 5 — *What is she looking for?*

Position 6 — *What should she do next?*

Homework

This is an exercise to do first thing in the morning.

Choose any spread that you like — lay out the cards and record them in your journal. Write down your first impressions, but save the interpretation until later.

Just before you go to bed, look at your journal and see what the spread might have meant that day. Hindsight provides great insight. You'll be able to see how accurate the reading was, how the cards describe your life, and the ways that you relate to the cards.

DESIGNING

Design Your Own Cards

By now you've had a lot of experience and practice with the Tarot. It's not old hat, but it feels comfortable (like wearing your pj's, sitting in a big armchair and sipping hot chocolate — or maybe not). You can look at a spread and see where the story is going. When you examine each individual card, you know how to tie it into its position (even without knowing the question). A dozen times a day you see something that relates to the Tarot. A friend tells you about a trip she is taking and the Eight of Wands comes to mind. A teacher offers advice for a problem and you're "this close" to calling him a Hierophant. It's at this point that you may decide to take your experience one step further.

More than creating your own spreads or opening statement, when you design your own cards you're changing your entire experience. It becomes intensely personalized, as the cards are your own view into the insight of the Tarot. This is not an exercise for a new Reader. As you can imagine, you'll need to know a great deal about the Tarot. And please remember that there are 78 cards in the deck, so this isn't an overnight project!

One of the reasons that Tarot cards work for a wide variety of people is that their symbols are universal. They are designed to reach beyond age, gender, culture, class, and religion. Most likely, the cards you create won't serve this function — which is all right. The idea is to personalize the experience — not broaden it.

The cards contain prompts — signals that will help you make that leap to the next level. When you learned the art of the Tarot, you followed someone else's (however well planned) prompts. It's your turn now. Remember the "ars memorativa" and develop your own system of clues and symbols. You will find this project to be (much like life and the Tarot itself) made up of opposing forces. On one hand, it requires a great deal of work and patience to finish the task. On the other, when you have the deck in hand, it will feel as natural as breathing.

You don't have to work exclusively with pictures. Include words or phrases if they help. The problem with words is that they are often too limiting. If you write the word "dog," the image it brings to mind is a dog — pure and simple. If you draw a picture of a dog riding a unicycle and juggling bones, we see playfulness, boundless energy, freedom, silliness and responding to the animal side of nature, which lets us be more instinctual and not so concerned about what others think.

That's the picture as a whole. Now break it up into pieces and respond to each bit. The dog, the unicycle, and the juggling all carry their own significance. This is another of the reasons that pictures are used rather than words — it is much easier to convey meaning within meaning. One picture can say something that would take paragraphs to explain.

If there is a word or phrase, that suits you, and is just the prompt you'll need, then by all means use it. These cards are for you. Perhaps "dog" says it all and sends you to the appropriate place. You could step it up a notch, though, by saying "Ginger" instead. (Let's say you had a dog named Ginger.) Writing "dog" is general and "Ginger" is specific. It says loyalty, love, and a creature who stuck by you through thick and thin. "Ginger" will remind you of all that plus warm feelings and memories. You will now be able to put so much more into the reading.

Colors

Devise a plan for colors. This will signal the significance of the card to you in a more subtle way. You won't need a special color to represent every emotion or intention (nor does a color have to represent something every time it appears on a card). You will find it useful, however, to know that red is a sign of action, or passion, or whatever you think is best. Keep the list short, though. If you assign meanings to 20 or 30 colors (everything from chartreuse to sea foam), you'll only make things more complicated. Trust yourself. You don't need all the answers in front of you. All you need is the tip of the iceberg and you'll know everything that's hiding underneath.

Reversed Readings

Does all of this seem confusing yet? Sorry, we're about to add one more element. Don't worry, though, it's more of a consideration than an actual task.

Remember that everything you've designed to be read in the upright position also has a reversed meaning. You don't have to draw or include anything that is relevant only to the reverse (though you can, by all means), but keep this in mind as you make up your design.

Ginger in reverse may remind you of the time she ate your shoes or ripped apart your favorite stuffed animal. Or when she ran away and was gone for two days — that didn't feel like loyalty — it just made you sad.

So, the point is that any picture, work, or phrase you include needs to have a possible opposite meaning. Something that will translate well for you with either reading.

Card Deck — Step-by-step

1. If you decide that you're ready to make your own deck, don't wake up the next day and start cutting, pasting, and coloring. It's something that you need to keep in mind for a while.

2. Start a dedicated journal to collect your thoughts and observations, clippings, and sketches. Include not just what has happened during readings, but things you've seen and experienced in your daily life.

3. Go through your old Tarot journal. Look for moments or comments that stand out. Copy these into your new design journal.

4. Start with the Major Arcana. Assign at least one page to each card. What characteristics do you think represent the Fool? After all the time that you've spent with the Fool, encountering him in surprising places and listening to his advice, you must have a few thoughts of your own about what part he plays in your life. Work your way from the Fool to the World.

5. Now, it's time for the Minor Arcana. Once again, move from beginning to end so you can work with the flow and cycle of each suit. One page — or half a page — will probably be enough. Decide for yourself. Follow the same procedure you did for the Major Arcana.

6. Use cardboard or stiff paper — maybe pages from an art sketch book — to create 78 different cards. Consider this a practice run so you can see how well the cards you've planned will work when finished. They don't have to be full color or complete designs. Just make sure that they contain all the components you've planned. Try a few spreads. Does it feel like anything is missing? Do your cards require any adjustments?

7. Finding the right materials to use is the next important step. You will need something that will last, is comfortable in your hands, and shuffles well. There is a brand of Tarot cards you can buy that are blank, but you may want to consider other options.

Go to an art supply or craft store. Have a look at the paper that is available. Find the one that suits you best. You can even choose different kinds that you can glue together. You might be able to find blank cards that are just the right size. Use your imagination. When you are finished, you might have your cards laminated.

8. Cut your paper (if necessary) into 78 cards and set to work. As always, start with the Fool. By this time, you'll know what you want on each one. Don't feel rushed.

9. What would you like on the back of the cards? You can leave them blank if you'd like, or use a single color to cover them. If you decide to use a design or picture, keep in mind that you don't want to give away the direction of the card itself — whether it will appear in the upright or reversed position in the spread. Use something that keeps the position of the card a mystery.

10. You've done it! Congratulations!

Double Team

If you have a friend who is also involved in the Tarot, you might want to design a deck together. You could each produce 39 cards.

1. Plan out the symbols for each card. Make a list of everything each card should contain.

2. Go off on your own and produce some sketches. Show them to each other to make sure you agree — this isn't the kind of project that you want to second-guess afterwards.

3. Gather all your materials and start working on your final draft.

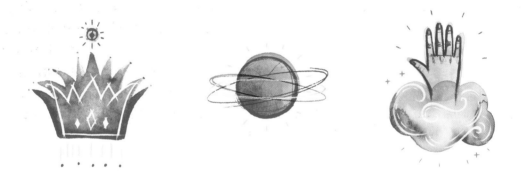

A good idea to keep you both involved with each card is having one draw the sketches and the other color them in. Take your assigned 39 cards and sketch the images and prompts that you have agreed upon. Your partner will do the same. Now, trade cards.

One of the most important aspects — if you want the experience to turn out well — is trust. You will need faith that your friend will produce cards and colors that you will appreciate and enjoy.

You might decide to reveal your Tarot journal to your partner, and this may not be an easy thing to do. It takes a great deal of trust to let someone in on your private thoughts. Or you could both sit and brainstorm ideas — each of you using your own journals as inspiration — until you've covered all the bases.

Design a Home for Your Cards

More than likely you will now want to keep your new deck someplace special. This could be something you find or that you design yourself. Personal expression is what matters here.

We've already discussed ways to design your own spreads as well as the cards themselves. By this point, you probably understand how to gather your thoughts and decorate things with images you create or ones you've collected. When it comes time to decorate your own bag or box for storing your cards, keep these ideas in mind and work your usual magic.

If you decide that you'd rather keep your cards in a box — something other than the one they came in — it's up to you to seek out one more suitable or build one yourself. In either case, one of the first things you need to consider is size. How well will your cards fit? They need to remain steady — or at least not falling loose in the box. If you open the box and your cards are scattered and out of place, you'll have to rethink the space issue. You could create a cushion or extra lining if you want to keep the container you have. This might be a nice idea — having a special bed to lay your cards in. The deck itself, as said before, should ideally be wrapped in natural fiber — like cotton or silk — but you can modify this if you find something else that you like a great deal.

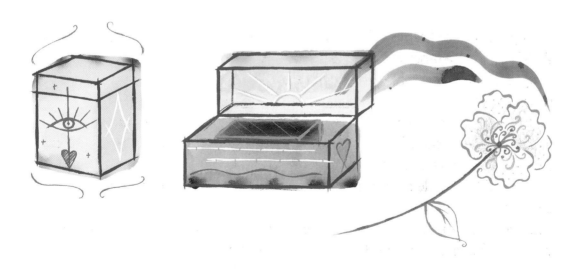

Card Box

When it comes to designing or decorating your storage box, you'll have more room to go a little wild — if only because you're probably using a stronger material. Try papier maché with newspaper or decoupage with colored paper (maybe paper that you've made). Paint it. Use crayons or magic markers — anything that's available — to cover the box, or leave it blank.

Card Bag

When it comes to a bag, you might find something already made that would work for you — maybe you'll find it in a store or your mother gave it to you years ago — you'll know when you find something extra special. It's probably best to avoid using things like an old sock — even if it is made from natural fiber. It would have to be a very special sock if it's going to hold your Tarot cards. A sock puppet — okay. A sock that you stole from your brother's dresser — forget it.

Another idea that will work well is to make the bag yourself. If you're a sewing expert — a seamstress/costume genius — you probably already have an elaborate idea to work on. Everyone else can keep it pretty simple and still have a very fine bag to house the deck.

Find a piece of cloth that appeals to you. Consider color, texture, and design — it's something you'll be looking at a lot. Don't just take the first thing you see.

There are several ways you can decorate the material itself. You could find patches, decals, or buttons to sew onto it. Can you do needlepoint? Maybe you can use that skill here. Or you might stitch your initials into the side of the bag, or embroider your favorite flower. Create a design with different colors of thread. You can do any of these before you sew your bag together or after it is finished. It can be always a work in progress.

Making Your Own Tarot Card Bag

Now, here are a few easy steps for making your own Tarot card bag:

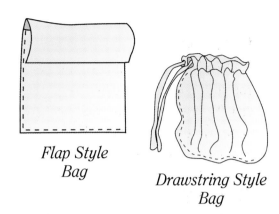

Flap Style Bag

Drawstring Style Bag

1. You'll need to have a rectangle of material at least 2 ½ times wider and a few inches taller than the cards. It doesn't have to be too big — remember that you can scale down, if need be, but it's difficult to add more. Decide which side of the cloth you want as the outside of the bag. Place the cloth down on a flat surface with the outside facing up (Fig. 1).

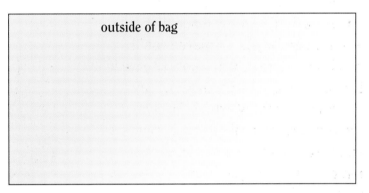

outside of bag

Figure 1

2. Lay your cards on the cloth, left of center, near the bottom edge, to see how much space you'll need. You'll want enough room to keep the deck snug without making it too difficult to get it in and out (Fig. 2).

3. Fold the cloth over the cards so the two edges line up. Now the inside of the cloth is facing you on the folded-over portion. You want to mark

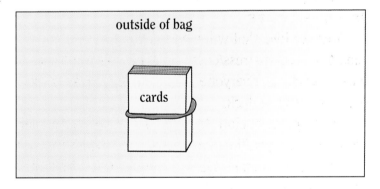

outside of bag

cards

Figure 2

the cloth (make sure you write on the inside) where you want to cut it. Will the inside of the cloth show pencil marks? If not, maybe there is some sewing chalk available that you can use. It will show up on most cloth.

Leave enough space along the bottom and left (the right side is the fold of the cloth) to stitch the cloth together. Leave extra room at the top. Now cut along the marked cut line (Fig. 3).

4. Open the cloth out to its full width. Decide how you want to close the bag — with a drawstring or a flap. If you want the flap closure, follow Steps a, b, c, and d below. If you want a drawstring closure, skip to Step e on page 120.

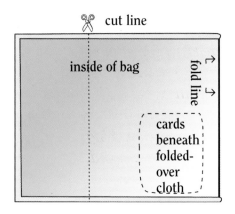

Figure 3

FLAP STYLE BAG:

a. If you would like the top to fold over and clasp shut, leave extra room at the top. With chalk, mark the line that will indicate the top of the bag and the beginning of the flap. Mark the middle fold line of the rectangle. Cut along the middle fold line until you reach the flap fold line (Fig. 4a).

Figure 4a

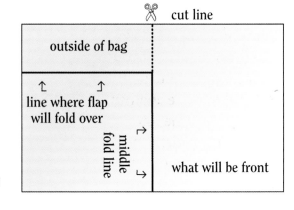

Mark a horizontal line on the right side of the rectangle. This line should be about half an inch above the flap fold line, because you will need to sew a hem (Fig. 4b). This will be the front of the bag. Then cut along the horizontal line across the front. Figure 4c shows the bag after cutting.

b. You will need to hem the top on the front side, so the material doesn't fray. If you want to sew the hem together (which means you will see the seam), fold the hem towards the inside front of the bag so the insides touch each other — the outside of the cloth will be exposed to you. Stitch along the hemline to the edge.

Note: *You can use fabric glue rather than needle and thread, which eliminates any problem with seeing the thread line. If you do this, fold the hem in so the insides are touching and the outside is exposed to you. Then glue the two insides together. Make sure you read the instructions on the glue bottle carefully before you start working.*

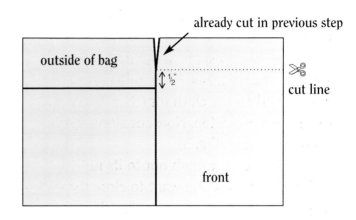

Figure 4b

c. Decide how tall the top flap needs to be. Cut it to the desired size, keeping in mind that you want to leave enough material to make another small hem on the top edge. Glue or stitch the hem on the inside of the bag (Fig. 4d).

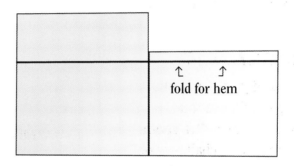

Figure 4c

d. What will you use to fasten the bag shut? You can buy Velcro, or snap-on buttons that can be glued or sewn onto the material. (If you choose to use real buttons, you will have to contend with making buttonholes, which is considerably harder.) Measure the distance needed from the edge of the top flap and attach the top part of the fastener inside the flap.

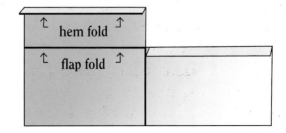

Figure 4d

Carefully measure where the bottom half of the fastener should be positioned on the front of the bag, and attach it (Fig. 4e). Go to Step 5 to finish the bag.

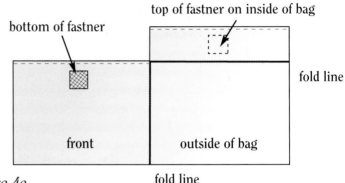

Figure 4e

DRAWSTRING STYLE BAG:

e. If you would rather use a drawstring to close the bag instead of a flap and Velcro or a button, you will, of course, need to find a cord. Decide how tall you would like the bag to be and draw a line across the rectangle to mark off the excess fabric, but be sure to leave enough for a hem. The hem should be wide enough for a cord to fit through it easily, but not so wide that it sags (Fig. 5a). Cut along the marked line.

Figure 5a

Note: *If you are gluing, you'll need a little extra material to fold over in order to glue it securely and have enough room for a tunnel for the cord.*

f. Now, sew or glue the hem edge down — inside to inside. Make sure that both ends of the hem are still open. Don't sew them shut (Fig. 5b).

g. Wait until you've finished assembling the bag before inserting the cord. Then attach a safety pin to one end of the cord. Insert the pin with cord attached into one end of the tunnel. You'll be able to slide the pin through the fabric tunnel of the hem and exit on the other side. The cord will follow (since it is attached to the pin), and your drawstring is ready to go. Tie the two ends of the drawstring together,

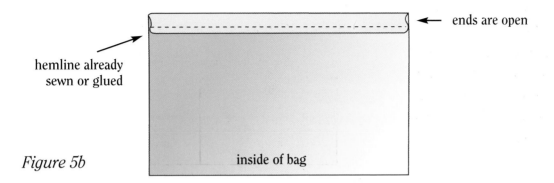

hemline already
sewn or glued

ends are open

inside of bag

Figure 5b

or tie large knots in the ends so they can't slip into the tunnel when you open the bag.

5. FOR EITHER STYLE OF BAG: Fold the back of the bag behind the front, with inside of fabric facing out. Line up the edges at the bottom and side, and pin in place. When stitching — or gluing — together the sides and bottom of bag — keep the bag turned inside out. This will make the seams less visible. It's probably a good idea to pin the sides together first so they don't pucker or gather. This will also keep the edges straight. Figures 6a and 6b show the flap-style closure. Figure 7a and 7b show the drawstring style.

Note: If your bag has a flap at the top, you obviously stop sewing/gluing when you reach the flap part.

Figure 6a

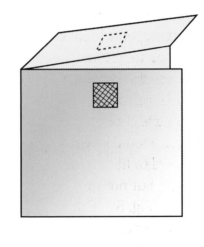

Figure 6b

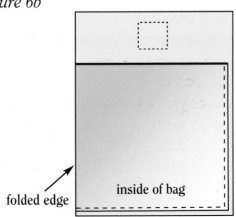

folded edge

inside of bag

If you are using a drawstring, make sure that you don't stitch up the ends that are meant to hold the cord — that would defeat the purpose (Figs. 7a and 7b).

6. Turn the bag so the inside is right where it should be — inside. Pull the cord through or close the flap and you're ready to go. All you need now is your deck of Tarot cards.

If you have any other arts and crafts skills, you could put them to use. A knitted bag would work well; so would one that you crochet. A couple of granny squares stitched together would work well. And you can still choose between a drawstring or clasp top. One consideration: If you want a drawstring and will be carrying your cards a fair bit, be aware that the yarn of a knitted bag may stretch out of shape over time. You could solve this by sewing a lining into the bag so the cards won't weigh down the bag and it will last longer.

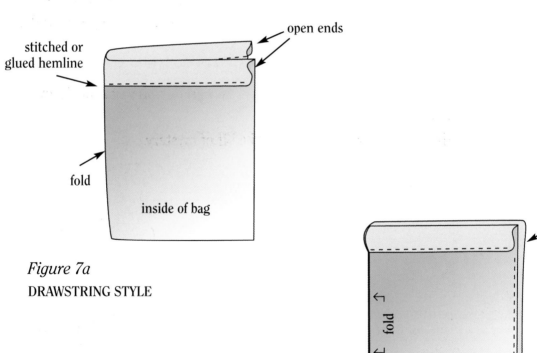

open ends

stitched or glued hemline

fold

inside of bag

Figure 7a
DRAWSTRING STYLE

open

fold

inside of bag

Figure 7b
DRAWSTRING STYLE

stitched or glued hem

Design Your Own Journal

You could start from the ground up by making the journal itself. Or you could use one that you've bought and decorate it. Find ways to make your journal uniquely yours — inside and out.

Outside

- ◆ Collect pictures and clippings that inspire you. Use these to decorate the outside of the journal. You can use one picture or many. You can create a collage or doodle on the pictures. Put your personal touch on them. You can add to your cover over time as you use the journal.

- ◆ Draw or paint something. There's nothing like personal artwork to adorn a private journal. You can plan a single picture to adorn the cover or fill the space with sketches and doodles. Copy your favorite images from the cards.

- ◆ Write poetry or words of inspiration.

- ◆ Inscribe a favorite reading on the cover to remind you what the Tarot can reveal.

- ◆ Leave the outside cover blank — add a bit of mystery.

Inside

This was covered, in part, in the previous section, "Keeping a Journal." By this time, you are probably familiar and comfortable with the process and know what works for you. Now that you've had experience with the cards, you'll know what is important to include in your journal. Should you divide the pages into columns? During your readings, are you inspired to write a lot of notes? Do you need to provide yourself extra space to record your thoughts? Do you need to include a section or space for later thoughts? There are numerous possibilities to consider, but only you will know what will work best or is necessary. Once you have set up your journal the way you want, you might consider ways to enliven the entries. A couple of ideas:

- ◆ Develop icons and short forms. Rather than use the words Upright, Reverse, Celebrate, Relationship, Love, Loss, etc., over and over, you can assign symbols to represent them.

- ◆ Use colors to distinguish categories. Red for cards read in reverse, blue for the upright position, and green for the outcome cards.

- ◆ Use your imagination and creativity to have fun with this project. Remember that your journal will one day be finished and you'll be starting a fresh one. You'll have plenty of time to revise old ideas and try out new ones. This is a renewable energy source that you will never extinguish.

If you enjoyed working with the Tarot — you're going to love. . .

Even though this is the end of the book, it isn't the end of all the things that could be said about the Tarot. There is always something else to learn and discover. The Tarot is too layered and varied (and, frankly, personal), for all its components to be covered in one book. Seek out books on astrology, the Kabbalah, philosophies surrounding the four elements, or numerology. If you're interested in the history of the Tarot, read about the Medieval French and Italian courts, the Crusades and the various orders — Templars, Masons, Rosicrucians, and the Order of the Golden Dawn. Learn about the history of the Gypsies, the Cathars, and old trade routes through the "new world." One topic will surely lead to another and they will all be beneficial to your Tarot journey. Enjoy your travels!

Important Words to Remember

A.E. Waite   Author of the Rider Tarot deck (used in this book).

Arcana   (pronounced ar-KAN-uh)   From the Latin word Arcanum meaning "secret."

Ars memorativa   The "art of memory" or mnemonics, based on the theory that pictures following a specific order will spark memory.

Celtic Cross   A traditional Tarot spread — one of the most popular.

Destiny Cards   The Trump cards of the Major Arcana. Called "destiny" cards because they deal with the larger issues in life that are more difficult to avoid.

Divinatory   Cards read in the upright position. Represents kinetic energy or energy in motion.

Elements (4)   Earth, Air, Water, and Fire.

Esoteric   Secret knowledge meant only for the initiated, confidential.

Free Will Cards   Cards of the Minor Arcana. They represent challenges or achievements that you can affect or change with action.

Gnostic   (pronounced nos-tik)   From the Greek, meaning "someone who knows." Having esoteric spiritual knowledge. Christian heretics of the 1st–3rd centuries.

Kabbalah   An encoded text of Jewish mystical thought.

Major Arcana   22 cards known as the Trumps or Destiny cards.

Minor Arcana   56 cards known as the "Free Will" cards.

Outcome Card   Usually the last card in a spread. Represents the final thought or culmination of the cards in a reading.

Querent   The person who asks the Tarot the question. Not always the same as the Reader.

Reverse Reading   Cards that are upside down and read in that position, representing potential, or energy at rest.

Rider-Waite deck   The most famous and widely used of all Tarot decks, also known as the Universal Waite or the Waite-Smith deck (for its designer, Pamela Coleman Smith), and *The Pictorial Key to the Tarot*.

Rosicrucians   Members of a society devoted to occult lore.

Significator   A card chosen by Querents to represent themselves in the reading.

Spreads   A specific pattern the Tarot cards follow to focus energy on the question asked. There is an endless number of possible spreads or layouts.

Tarocchi   An early Italian card game. It's believed that this is one of the roots of word "Tarot."

Tree of Life   Encoded language of the Jewish mystical text, the Kabbalah.

Trump Cards   Another term for cards in the Major Arcana.

Index